Solitude and Love of the World

*Other Books by Thomas Merton
published by Burns & Oates*

THE ASCENT TO TRUTH
BREAD IN THE WILDERNESS
CONJECTURES OF A GUILTY BYSTANDER
THE LIVING BREAD
THE NEW MAN
NO MAN IS AN ISLAND
RAIDS ON THE UNSPEAKABLE
THOUGHTS IN SOLITUDE
THOUGHTS ON THE EAST
THE WAY OF CHUANG TZU
THE WISDOM OF THE DESERT

Also published by Burns & Oates

John Howard Griffin
THOMAS MERTON: THE HERMITAGE YEARS

SOLITUDE AND LOVE OF THE WORLD

Thomas Merton

With a Foreword by
ROLAND WALLS

BURNS & OATES

BURNS & OATES
Wellwood, North Farm Road,
Tunbridge Wells, Kent TN2 3DR

This edition first published in Great Britain 1997

The essays in this book were first published in
Contemplation in a World of Action in 1971.

ISBN 0 86012 278 6

Typeset by Search Press Limited
Printed and bound in Great Britain by
Biddles Ltd, Guilford and King's Lynn

Contents

Foreword

Thomas Merton of the *Seven Storey Mountain* emerged out of his chrysalis to become a radical critic of a fossilized monastic tradition that he considered had lost its fire and its vision, and could cause death of the soul. He then flew off to his hermitage in the monastery grounds, and later, at the end of his life, he literally flew to Bangkok, to his death. In life and even in death he was a modern man. He died after taking a shower and then touching a faulty electric heater. He died leaving a series of dots . . . leaving an enigma as to where next.

The drive of this strange trajectory was his obsession with the relation of God to the world God loved. He traced this relation to roots in himself, his vocation to live in solitude, and his seemingly opposite call to live fully open to the miseries and follies of twentieth-century life. He was a radical. He was a radical hermit who, in solitude with God and his own complex psyche, lived out his life sharing the radical love of God's love of his world. He was a radical prophet with a message to the world, and therefore to the Church, the servant of both the Word and the world.

Merton's obsession with the need for an infusion of a radical prophetic element into the seemingly fading contemplative life (at least in vocations to contemplative Orders) marks his essay "Is the contemplative life finished?" It was written after the short spring after the war, when new foundations sprang up all over the U.S.A. Merton directed his attention, not to the secondary problem of monastic life, the reform of structures; he went deeper to consider the very nature of contemplation: if it meant, as it did for many, the alienation of the monk from the world, then Marx was right. Yes, the vocation is to renounce oneself and one's

7

selfish use of and joining a selfish world. It did not mean a flight of the "alone to the Alone." It did not mean the abandonment of the wretchedness of the world, nor of the joys of human love, of art or of secular literature. The *unum necessarium* is not found that way, but by a renunciation of self-love and a recovery of the love of God and of his love and compassion for the human race—to be drawn into the love of God for himself, and therefore into God's essential concern for humanity and for the planet he created. Contemplative life can only survive and recover its true centre and circumference if this is done.

There are two questions we might ask Merton. First, is he really correct in encouraging the imagination, even with consecrated discipline? Most contemplatives I have spoken to, especially those who take Merton's point about prophetic contemplation, do not follow him here. They follow St John of the Cross in imageless prayer. They find the way of pure love a better way of entering into God's boundless love for us and his universe. One could be forgiven for thinking that Merton had justified his own exuberant imagination rather than undertake a rigorous examination of the tradition. Secondly, is he too engaged in the monastic tradition to take on board the real phenomenon beginning to manifest itself then, and, of course, more than ever today—the amazing growth of vocations to heart prayer among the laity, married and single, often living busy lives in the world? Dag Hammarskjöld managed it in a very busy life.

Merton would have been surprised at what has happened since his death in 1968, at least by the recognition and affirmation of the hermit vocation and its place in the life of the Church. Since then there has been a remarkable increase in the number of hermits, male and female, priest and lay, internationally and denominationally, solitary or in small groups (*lauras*). By 1975 a conference of hermits was held at St David's, Wales: they came from Britain and Europe; they

represented Orthodox, Catholic, Anglican, and Congrega-
tionalist traditions, and the papers were collected into a
book, *Solitude and Communion* (Fairacres Publications).

In 1983 the Code of the New Canon Law (in Canon 603)
clarified the place of the hermit life in the Roman Catholic
Church. It recognized hermits as dedicated to God in the
consecrated life "if they publicly professed the evangelical
counsels and then led their form of life under the diocesan
bishop." In 1996 Pope John Paul II issued his Apostolic
Exhortation *Vita Consecrata*. In it he commended the new
emergence of eremitical life, so long dormant in the West.
"Men and women hermits belonging to the ancient Orders
or new Institutes, or being dependent on the bishop, bear
witness to the passing of the present age by their inward and
outward separation from the world. By fasting and peni-
tence they show that man does not live by bread alone but
by the Word of God. Such a life in the desert is an invitation to their contemporaries and to the ecclesial community
itself never to lose sight of the supreme vocation which is
always to be with the Lord" (para. 70).

It is not so easy to record how far this ecumenical and
official embrace of this form of life has taken on Merton's
supreme interest in the "worldliness" of this essential prophetic world-renunciation, or whether the hermits themselves have been exploring Merton's insights. Perhaps a particular incident at the St David's Conference will help to
explain that it is still alive, and also illustrate the issue at the
forefront of Merton's mind. Halfway through the conference, an Anglican nun-hermit asked me for a second opinion about what was happening to her after seven years of
eremitic life. She told me she was experiencing a strange
shift in her prayer and consciousness. When she first became a hermit she was primarily focussing on God and his
Church. Now the Church was fading from the centre, the
only focus was God and creation with all the human race

and their union in Christ. I told her that I thought this could be God moving her to centre on the greatest mystery of his love—his love for the world. Her eremitic life had expanded her consciousness, to ponder and enter the mystery of the Incarnation—"the Word was made flesh," "the Son was made man"—not a Christian, not a Catholic, not an Anglican, but man for the salvation of us all. I then asked her what her director had told her. She replied, "The same thing in almost the same words." How delighted Merton would have been to have heard that!

Other evidence for renewed interest in the eremitical life is hidden away in periodicals of religious Orders. There is an ever-growing ferment among them about how to return to the specific charism of some founders, among the Benedictines, Cistercians, Carmelites, and Franciscans in particular. There is a growing request from old and new brothers and sisters for at least periods of solitude and return to the desert, to recover poverty and simplicity, the family form over against organization, insecurity over against well-cushioned financial security, and the like.

One must also add the increasing monastic and eremetic dimension in interface dialogue. There is a wish on both sides to share, compare, and contrast each tradition's experience of silence and solitude among Christians, Buddhists, and Hindus. This move into sharing experiences is building on the previous attempts in the early part of this century by Fr Jules Monchanin and Fr Henri de Seaux and later by Fr Bede Griffiths and his ashram in India. This development links up with Merton and his *Asian Journal*. Parts of the journal are an extremely valuable account of his inward struggles with his own rich and complex personality as he grew in self-knowledge. He had the never-ending task of harnessing his dominant self to the goal of self-forgetfulness. His writings have the authenticity that belongs to one who has lived it all on the pulse. He warns us not to be deceived by the pious rhetoric with which glib books and retreat addresses betray that even their authors don't believe in their own spiritual hype. Merton has a healthy fear of deceiving himself or anyone else. He is looking you in the eye as he writes.

The core of Merton's thought is about the prophetic sign the hermit is to be. It is the sign of complete insecurity, basic nakedness of human life; he/she shares the poverty of the human condition, entirely dependent as every man and woman is on God, though it is hardly ever acknowledged. Such a sign of the human condition will mean the hermit is always a bit of a conundrum to society and also to the Church in the situation of comfortable activity. S/he is an offence to the do-gooders and to religious people alike. S/he escapes both the managed and the managerial society. Merton knows by experience and can describe this double journey towards his own bare humanity and towards the new humanity recreated by and in Christ. The solitary is "free from the exorbitant demands of society and institutions." Without faith such a life "could not possibly make sense." Yet it is not achieved by the fanatic and certainly not by the legalist, and never by the tepid and lukewarm. What I find so attractive in so much of Merton is his persistent, down-to-earth, common sense of a Christian humanist. He releases us from the tedium of self-concerned, anxious "spirituality," from churchiness that so often ducks the demands which Christ's love makes on us.

He underlines the Desert tradition of the *Abba* in the sense of spiritual guide (though he did not make use of it himself)—a guide so necessary in a life in which one can easily substitute the insidious desires of the deceived and deceiving heart, as it lures us into self-pleasing and self concern, for self-consecration. Wakefulness, watchfulness, is all. He also writes of the use and meaning of the Cell, of the need for relaxation in music, light reading, or art. Merton excels in balancing freedom of the Spirit and the need for order and discipline. He combined his solitude with an articulate apostolate in books, letter-writing and an obviously enjoyed welcome of guests to his cell, and latterly with a long journey to Bangkok. Such open-ended hermit life would have suited his many-sided temperament and his ever-increasing involvement in the prophetic, always against the stream, in criticism of a Church and world structured for comfort, property, power and status. All of these kill prophecy.

Merton warned against the ever-present dangers of professionalism in monasticism and hermit life: "Contemplative is a bad word." It leads to exclusivism, to a special perch in ecclesiastical life. It gives itself airs and graces, obstructing the call to be a sign of contradiction, a sign of the utter nakedness of the human condition which we spend so much time covering up. Then dependence on God becomes a pious non-experienced cliché instead of a discovered reality. The hermit should be a threat to an easy-going, cosy activity, a threat to anyone imprisoned in churchy religionism in a world crying out for God.

ROLAND WALLS
Hermitage of the Transfiguration, Scotland
May 1997

CHRISTIAN SOLITUDE

Christian Solitude

Christians are emerging from an era of individualistic piety. The new emphasis on the communal brotherly life of those who have been called to oneness in Christ is in fact a liberation from a narrow, self-preoccupied struggle for a perfection too evidently tinged with narcissism. An individualistic quest of "contemplation" has often resulted, in fact, in fanciful regression to a tepid womb of oceanic feelings. The reaction against individualism has therefore not only revived the Christian sense of solidarity in love, work, and responsibility, but has brought us a new realization of the meaning of the person. This in its turn has meant a new awareness of the seriousness of solitude, not simply as an expression of man's existential plight, but as a Christian value, a challenge, and even as a vocation.

The Christian life is to be seen dialectically, not only as a communal effort from which solitude is ostracized nor as a lonely pilgrimage without fraternal solidarity, but as a growth in one "Mystical Person," one Christ, in whom the solitude and independence of the person develop together with his capacity for love and commitment. Scholars have at the same time drawn attention to the importance of the wilderness theme, the desert pilgrimage, in the Bible and in the whole history of theological thought.

So now, in the Catholic Church, in liturgy and in theology, while we are rediscovering the meaning of oneness as the People of God, we are also becoming aware of the fact that we are a pilgrim community travelling in the wilderness under the guidance of God, and that some members of the Holy People are bound to have a special consciousness of this wilderness and exiled aspect of the Christian life. Unless we are fully aware of the seriousness of solitude and the isolation and anguish of the person without love, our protestations of joy, hope, and communal fervour may ring dreadfully hollow in the ears of those who know the absurdity of shallow optimism.

This preoccupation with the person and his solitude is nothing new. The Christian existentialists have had a lot to say about it, and though they are perhaps not now as fashionable as they were in the 1950s, their reflections about man in mass society have not lost any of their point. The idea of alienation remains one of the keys to our social and psychological predicament. We know that we live in a society which needs large numbers of its members to be alienated, and which also needs slums into which it can dump those who, for one reason or another, cannot face up to the competition of living affluently. One function of the slum is to isolate the outcast not only from the rest of society but even from the other outcasts around him. The slum is the equivalent of the desert wilderness today—hence, the new quasi-monastic families, like the Little Brothers of Jesus, which began in the Sahara, and have gravitated to the slums of Paris or Detroit or to the *poblaciones* of South America. The slum is now the abode of utter loneliness, risk, helplessness—a true desert. Yet it is massively overcrowded—a tragic and unnatural solitude.

While there still remain solitudes—woods, mountains, and islands—the monastic charism will still summon a few men to live there alone, for one reason or another.

The monastic life is by definition solitary. True, its ordinary shape in modern times is communal, but even then the monastery is always a kind of wilderness community—as was Qumran. There is always an element of perilous ambiguity in monastic theories that glorify the communal life of the monastery as if it were the ideal pattern for the Christian community. The basis of human and Christian community is marriage, and celibate communities are something beyond the normal—and we are well aware of the harm done by attempting to impose a monastic style of spirituality on the lay Christian. The monk was originally a *layman* (priests were exceptional) who lived alone in the desert outside the framework of any institution, even of the Christian and ecclesial institution. His state was consciously *abnormal*—therefore a state of penitent mourning. His loneliness had a prophetic and mysterious quality, something almost in the nature of a sacramental sign, because it was a particular charismatic way of participating in the death and resurrection of Christ.

What is lonelier than death? To confront the emptiness, the void, the apparent hopelessness of this desert and to encounter there the miracle of new life in Christ, the joy of eschatological hope already fulfilled in mystery—this was the monastic vocation. Hence *real* loneliness, real conditions of emptiness and deprivation were required. A mere intention of solitude could not suffice.

Kierkegaard used to illustrate the fact that "Christian values" could become very abstract by the story of a man who said he was going to the North Pole and then went for a walk around the block. Some of the unrest in contemporary monasticism is due to the fact that monastic values have too often degenerated into such walks round the block. The monastery today tends to be a busy village, and life can become as organized, as noisy and as fussy as anywhere else. Provided a monk remains within the walls, keeps the rule of silence moderately well, and strives for a certain "recollection," he is supposed to tell himself that he is "alone" when in fact he is jostling along in a small agitated crowd. Obviously in such circumstances many will feel more honest if they abandon the pretence, and decide to talk to one another and get along as an authentic group. This is one of the directions being taken by monastic renewal at the present. But unless this is balanced by opportunities for physical solitude, it will only result in the monastic life becoming more busy and more futile than ever. (Note: Statements like these imply a lot that the reader may or may not be taking for granted. In all forms of communal life we tend to multiply useless activities—time-consuming obsessions which for psychological reasons we are unable to abandon. Pascal saw this so well and described it as man's insatiate need to escape himself in movement, diversion: "Hence it is that men so much love noise and stir . . . hence it is that the pleasure of solitude is a thing so incomprehensible.")

So, in the monastic Orders, provision is now made for the monks to go into solitude temporarily or even permanently, where the circumstances permit. This means that several monasteries now have monks living in the woods, near the monastery, as hermits. Such experiments are going on in the Cistercian monasteries in Kentucky, South Carolina, and Utah, and also at the Primitive Benedictine foundation at Abiquiu in New Mexico. In addition to this, there is the hermit colony founded recently in British Columbia by Dom Jacques Winandy, a retired Benedictine Abbot (from Clervaux in Luxembourg) and peopled by former Benedictine and Cistercian monks.

A place has thus been made for Christian eremitical solitude within the monastic institution. This is of course a very welcome development. On the other hand, the situation is not without its ambiguities. They must not be ignored. And yet it is very hard to clarify them. The whole question of eremitism has been kept deliberately out of sight for years, and its problems and possibilities have not yet been seriously studied. There is always a danger that those who are now experimenting with it may be tacitly expected to prove themselves perfect models: "All right, you wanted this, so presumably you know what it is all about. We are waiting for you to show us!" But show what? Models of what? These expectations may be loaded with tacit demands that cannot be and should not be met. For instance: must the modern monastic hermit prove himself to be a replica of some Egyptian or Syrian Desert Father of the fourth century? Well, hardly. To begin with, Desert Father stories fall into a special literary form which admits and indeed requires a generous element of distortion—an apparent inhumanity which, on closer examination, proves to be compensated by other distortions in the opposite sense. This balance of distortions is typical of *apothegmata* and *fioretti*. The first function of a modern hermitage would seem to be quite the opposite: to relax and to heal and to smooth out one's distortions and inhumanities.

Whereas in the fourth century monks were determined to prove their solitude charismatic by showing it to be beyond the human, the situation today is quite the reverse. The whole of man's life is now pushed to extremes pressing him almost to his biological and psychological limit. Hence the mission of the solitary is first the full recovery of man's human and natural measure. Not that the solitary merely recalls the rest of men to an impossible Eden. But he reminds them of what is theirs to use if they can manage to extricate themselves from the web of myths and fixations which a highly artificial society has imposed on them. The hermit exists today to realize and experience in himself the ordinary values of a life lived with a minimum of artificiality. Such a life will from the beginning seem itself artificial, because it is so completely unlike the lives of other people. The hermit will be accused of being the most contrived of all simply because he does not float away on the immense tide of artificiality with everybody else. And of course, if he is too conscious of a revolutionary intent, if he tries to put himself on display as utterly different, he may well be nothing but an eccentric. That would be unfortunate—but it is not unavoidable. In any event, the Christian solitary should avoid all trappings and décor of a theatrical eremitism—the hood, the costume, the retinue of devoted birds and squirrels (though they will be around anyway), the diet of bread and water, the stone pillow, the rosary of knotted string, the bed of twigs. These things are affectations, and we might as well recognize that even the classification of "hermit" has its dangers.

The Christian solitary life today should bear witness to the fact that certain basic claims about solitude and peace are in fact true. And in doing this, it will restore people's confidence, first in their own humanity and beyond that in the grace of God.

The monastic hermit has, as his first duty, to live happily and without affectation in his solitude. He owes this not only to himself, but to the monastic community that has gone so far as to give him a chance to try it out. In fact, this is one of the specifically Christian and communal aspects of the experiment. The monastic hermit realizes that he owes his solitude to his community, and owes it in more ways than one. First of all, the community has bestowed it upon him, in an act of love and trust. Second, the community helps him to stay there and make a go of it, by prayers and by material aid. Finally, the hermit "owes his solitude" to the community in the sense that his solitary life with its depth of prayer and awareness is his contribution to the community, something that he gives back to his "monastic Church" in return for what has been given him.

This is very important, because in this way monastic solitude retains its fully communal and Christian character and is not a mere escape from collective tasks and limitations. To live happily and without affectation in solitude: this is the chief obligation of the monastic hermit because, as I said above, it can restore to others their faith in certain latent possibilities of nature and of grace. More especially it can, today, restore the faith of monks in one of the basic claims of the monastic vocation itself. If a monk can take literally the promise implicit in his vocation and find that by living entirely alone he can discover the values he came seeking when he first entered the monastery, then he will by his life affirm the truth that the values are there and that they are real. It would of course be most unrealistic to imagine that these values are to be found only, or mostly, in pure solitude. Anyone who had not been able to find them in the beginning of his communal life would probably never find them in solitude either.

To be more precise, the monastic vocation, like any other, is a call to a life of constant organic growth. One of the problems of a rigidly institutional monastic life in which everything is organized on one pattern for everyone is that growth may be frustrated.

If after fifteen or twenty years in the common life a monk can go to a hermitage, he can there create a new personal pattern which will fulfill his own special needs for growth. He is no longer at the mercy of a pattern devised for another. In Greek monasticism this has always been taken for granted. The granting of the "Great Habit" after many years established the mature monk in a fully contemplative life when he was finally ready for it—and did not assume that he became a contemplative on entering the novitiate.

Man is ever face to face with the inescapable spectres of boredom, futility, and madness. A healthy and well-organized social life enables man to cope with these spectres by fruitful work, love, and personal growth. The person who loves his ordinary life because his work is meaningful and because his relationship with those around him is joyful, open, and generous will never be bored. An unhealthy social system both exacerbates man's fear of boredom and exploits it. The modern American is kept in terror of boredom and unfulfillment because he is constantly being reminded of

21

their imminence—in order that he may be induced to do something that will exorcise him for the next half hour. Then the terror will rise up again and he will have to buy something else, or turn another switch, or open another bottle, or swallow another pill, or stick himself with a needle in order to keep from collapsing.

In the monastic life these escapes do not exist—they are not necessary. Yet in time of crisis and change there is a great deal of concern about making the monastic life more interesting, more rewarding, by improving the patterns, enlivening the observances, diminishing tensions. All this is of course necessary, but unfortunately it tends to develop into the same agitated flight from boredom which, everywhere else, makes boredom all the more inevitable. The trouble lies in assuming that there must be some kind of social machinery which, once discovered and set in motion, will remove everybody's problems. The anguished effort to construct this machinery and get it moving drives everybody wild.

In reality, no such machinery exists. Society can simply remove obstacles or make them negotiable. It remains for the person to make use of the opportunities thus provided, and lead his own life in a happy and fruitful manner— helping others to do the same.

The hermit is, or should be, happy without having a happiness machine to solve his problems for him. He faces boredom squarely *with no other resources than those he has within himself*—his own capacities and God's grace. He puts these resources to work, and discovers that his life is never boring. On the contrary, renouncing care and concern about getting somewhere and having fun, he finds that to live is to be happy, once one knows what it is to *live* in simplicity.

The hermitage then provides the monk with something that a mature person needs: the chance to explore, to risk, to abandon himself sagaciously to untried possibilities. This is one of the most important aspects of the wilderness theme in the Bible and in the history of the People of God. After all, it was in the desert and hazard of Sinai that the People of God acquired its identity, its full consciousness of the covenant relationship which the prophets later described as an "espousal" with Yahweh.

The Christian solitary, in his life of prayer and silence, explores the existential depths and possibilities of his own life by entering into the mystery of Christ's prayer and temptation in the desert, Christ's nights alone on the mountain, Christ's agony in the Garden, Christ's Transfiguration and Ascension. This is a dramatic way of saying that the Christian solitary is left alone with God to fight out the question of who he really is, to get rid of the impersonation, if any, that has still followed him into the woods. He thus receives from God his "new name," his mysterious identity in Christ and his Church. The one great advantage of the woods is that one cannot—at least sanely—play a part in them. Or if one manages to defy reality and continue in some fictitious "role," the result will quickly prove disastrous. At the same time, it is not altogether easy to be perfectly honest with oneself, and solitude brings this fact out. The wood may well foment new madnesses that one did not suspect before. But it would seem that solitude is not a satisfactory setting for concerted, thoroughgoing madness. To be really mad, you need other people. When you are by yourself you soon get tired of your craziness. It is too exhausting. It does not fit in with the eminent sanity of trees, birds, water, sky. You have to shut up and go about the business of living. The silence of the woods forces you to make a decision which the tensions and artificialities of society may help you to evade forever. Do you want to be yourself or don't you? Do you insist on fighting the images of other people? Must you continue to live as a symbolic appendage to somebody else you desire or hate? Are you going to stand on your own feet before God and the world and take full responsibility for your own life?

Of course, this decision must naturally be possible everywhere. Love makes it possible and imperative in social life. For some, marriage is what normally brings the decision to a head, or it should. I would say that for a few others, the call to solitude, accepted and fulfilled in joy, is the only real guarantee of their being finally born. If they respond to it, if they get born, if they become happy and are content just to be themselves and not impose themselves and their private idiocies on anybody else, they will do a signal service to the rest of mankind.

Extending to mankind as a whole what I said a moment ago about the monastic community, the solitary who manages to live happily because he knows he is finally born, or that he soon will be, restores to the rest of men some elementary hope that this basic need is not an illusion and that it can be fulfilled. The example of its fulfillment in solitude must not, of course, imply a claim that solitude is the only way. But the example of the solitary has a special usefulness. The grace of solitude is a grace of independence: a breaking away from certain exorbitant claims of society and of institutions. Society has a way of enlarging its demands to the point where it arrogates to itself complete power over everyone and everything. It tells you, in effect, "you not only need the love of other people, but you need to be completely enslaved and dominated by other people. You need not only to be in rapport with others, you need to be swallowed up by them." One of the things most wrong about the exaggerated legalism and institutionalism in the Catholic Church today is this attempt to dominate Christians by fear—the implication that if they do not submit to complete over-control they will cease to exist as true human beings and as members of Christ. This is so manifestly false that some Catholics are literally driven away from the visible Church in which they cannot, in conscience, meet some exorbitant demand stupidly forced on them by incompetent officials. The man who can live happily without snuggling up at every moment to some person, institution, or vice is there as a promise of freedom for the rest of men. And that perhaps is one of the only reasons why the solitary can be so bitterly resented, especially by a certain type of Christian for whom the Church is mere institution and womb.

What is the pattern of solitary life in this monastic setting? The hermit is bound to the Rule of St Benedict and to his monastic vows. He remains in obedience to his abbot, retains his status in his community, and lives according to a schedule which is roughly that of the other monks. But this is quite flexible. At Gethsemani the hermits (there are two) go to bed and get up about the same time as the community. They are both priests and both say Mass in a small chapel in the monastery. The two hermits live about a mile apart, in the woods. One of them still says the old Latin office, the other says his office in English. Both spend a certain amount of time in manual work, taking care of the hermitages and making their own living. One of them is more inclined to intellectual work than the other. He is also interested in Zen and Yoga. For recreation there are solitary walks in the woods and Thoreau's inspecting of snowstorms. Some contacts are maintained with the outside world. The hermit life does not necessarily demand absolute isolation: this too should be flexible and a matter of individual choice. There may be real reasons for a certain amount of limited correspondence, for a few visits and conversations. Obviously, however, there must be limits to all this, or solitude itself may once again be reduced to a mere abstraction.

How have people reacted to this experiment?

25

First of all, it has become a matter of routine and gossipy curiosity. This is understandable, but more or less irrelevant. It indicates a certain basis of acceptance without much understanding. The men who came to put up the electric line to one of the hermitages soon had it figured out in terms of "peace and quiet." In the books of the Rural Electric Cooperative the hermitage is billed as a "lodge" and there is a certain readiness to concede that the hermits would logically live on rabbits and other game, which in fact they do not.

Some of the local Protestant ministers and professors from the Southern Baptist Seminary in Louisville, who formerly used to meet and converse with one of the monks who became hermits, have regarded it as a regrettable withdrawal and have not been disposed to understand what it was all about. They have of course admitted the right of the one concerned to follow his own conscience in this barely comprehensible fashion.

On the other hand, people from India, Japan, North Africa (Hindus, Buddhists, and Muslims) have thoroughly understood the hermit idea and approved of it without difficulty, taking it for granted as an obvious development of the monastic life.

What is most important is of course the reaction of the monastic community itself. The hermits have been thoroughly accepted, and everyone seems happy about them. One of the routine arguments against hermits, put forth before the experiment, was that if one or two were allowed to live in the woods there would be a mad rush into solitude. "Everyone will be asking for a hermitage." This has not turned out to be the case. It is clear that most members of the community do not want to live permanently alone. Others who are still young in monastic life are content to wait their turn. Meanwhile, however, there will be more opportunities for temporary solitude and a hermitage may be built in which monks will be permitted to spend a day or two now and again, if they wish. This seems to be about as much solitude as most monks need. Their real vocation remains in the monastic community.

Relations between the hermits and the community are very happy. But this of course is not automatic. It is a question of real charity on both sides. In other words, the hermit does not vanish into a void but moves into a new and special relationship with the community. The relationship clearly has mutual obligations that need to be understood and observed with good sense as well as love. The future of the hermit experiment in some monasteries could easily be prejudiced by failures in this regard. Once again, the hermit must not be an eccentric and make such odd demands that he becomes a pest to the community. The grace of the solitary life in a monastic setting definitely implies a willingness for the hermit to mind his own business and for the community to mind theirs. This is fortunately being realized so far at Gethsemani. The spirit of mutual understanding, tolerance, and affection is quite marked. The hermits meanwhile continue to contribute to the community life in one way or another. One of them for instance gives one conference a week to those who are interested (about one third of the community attends). The hermits show up for concelebration on Sundays and big feasts. The cenobites meanwhile have been very good about staying away from the hermitages and leaving the hermits alone.

To sum it up: one feels at Gethsemani that as long as the hermits are thought to be quietly happy, the rest of the community will be happy with them. And if the hermits start getting too nutty, too demanding, too eccentric, or if they take it into their heads to try to run the community from the hermitage, this will hardly be appreciated. The elementary obligation of the hermit is to renounce all arbitrary demands on other people. The hermit's ability to live alone is his gift to the community and his witness to the grace of Christ in his own life. It is as simple as that, and he is accepted on that basis by the community.

There will probably always remain some nagging doubts that the hermit life might be self-centred. Some will say: "Sure! Why shouldn't the hermit be happy? He lives in his own little world! He is content because he is the sole possessor of a universe of which he is himself the centre." The most incredible thing about this statement is that anyone could accept it as a viable formula for happiness. The only possible answer is: "If you think you can be happy by doing that, why don't you just try it?" The fact is that this is a pure myth. Man is not made in such a way that he can live happily without love. If his life is centred on himself, he may indeed be able to function, but in order to do so his existence is necessarily complicated by his machinery for imposing his will on others. One cannot live a self-centred life *simply*. Too much cheating is involved—even if one only cheats oneself. Supposing a man does live self-centredly in solitude: he may manage to get by, but he will hardly be content. His discontent will obviously reach out and affect others in some way. He will be mean and unpleasant with them; he will act out his obsessions and inner frenzies upon them. He will project his self-hate on them. He will need them and use them for some irrational purpose, and they will be aware of the fact. Lovelessness cannot be kept hidden, because a loveless life is essentially unhappy, frustrated, and destructive.

The solitary life is then anything but "lonely"—if by loneliness is meant a loveless and abandoned state. The life of Christian solitude is before all else a life of love, a life of *special* love. And love is never abstract. It centres on a concrete, existential good, a value that is perceived and experienced as coming directly from the ground and source of all good—God's love for man in Christ. The solitary life of the Christian hermit is not simply a life in which one thinks about the good, but a life of total response to it, complete surrender to it, based on a personal and existential awareness that one is called into solitude by a special act of God's merciful love. It is a way of saying: "I have known and experienced the goodness of God to me in Christ in such a way that I have no alternative but this total response, this gift of myself to a life alone with God in the forest. And this witness is at the same time the purest act of love for other men, my gift to them, my contribution to their joy in the good news of Jesus Christ, and to their awareness that the Kingdom of Christ is in the midst of us."

The Christian solitary bears witness to his faith by his very solitude. Without faith such a life could not possibly make real sense. This is obvious to logic; for, if it is a life of love, the solitary life must have some way of remaining in contact with the good that is its object That way is faith, and faith only. It is by faith, as the author of Hebrews said, that the witnesses to God's revelation in Judaism risked their lives and survived when they roamed the deserts in sheepskins and goatskins (Heb. 11:37-8). It is by faith that the solitary knows himself loved and called by God into the wilderness. If he cannot always give a perfectly satisfactory reason for his faith to other men, that does not matter. What matters is the liveliness of his faith as it burns in his own heart.

Certainly the fact of moving to a hermitage does not turn a man instantly into a saint. He retains his human defects, he remains capable of failure and error, and like everyone else in such a case he depends on the understanding and love of his brothers, just as he gives them his own love and understanding in their own need. But the real structure of the Christian solitary vocation remains this: it is a response to a personal call from God in Christ. It is a life of love for

God based on faith, verified by the assent of the monastic community and supported by the loving care and understanding of that community. And it is in turn a contribution to the life and faith of the community and of the Church as a whole. Christian solitude is then essentially an expression of the mystery of the Church, even when in some sense it implies a certain freedom from institutional structures. But in the case of monastic eremitism, the solitary life retains a definite and approved institutional form. The hermit remains within the cadres of monastic obedience and community, while at the same time living a life of solitude and freedom "in the Spirit." His freedom is never a freedom from the Church but always a freedom in the Church and a contribution to the Church's own charismatic heritage.

THE CELL

The Cell

A brother asked one of the Elders saying: What shall I do, Father, for I work none of the works of a monk but here I am in torpor eating and drinking and sleeping and in bad thoughts and in plenty of trouble, going from one struggle to another and from thoughts to thoughts. Then the old man said: Just you stay in your cell and cope with all this as best you can without being disturbed by it. I would like to think that the little you are able to do is nevertheless not unlike the great things that Abba Antony did on the mountain, and I believe that if you sit in your cell for the Name of God and if you continue to seek the knowledge of him, you too will find yourself in the place of Abba Antony.[1]

This variant of a classic Desert Father saying emphasizes that the most important thing for the solitary is to be a solitary, to "sit in his cell" because the cell will "teach him all things." Everything else is secondary. The relative unimportance of all other practices is suggested by this hyperbolic and somewhat outrageous statement. We must not interpret this saying to mean that asceticism is discounted. But fasting, vigils, and so on are seen in their proper relation to solitude and prayer.

The right order of things in the solitary life is this: everything is centred on union with God in prayer and solitude. Therefore the most important "ascetic practice" is solitude itself, and "sitting" alone in the silence of the cell. This patient subjection to loneliness, emptiness, exile from the world of other men, and direct confrontation with the baffling mystery of God sets the tone, so to speak, for all other

---

1. An apothegm published by Nau, "Histoire des Solitaires Egyptiens," *Revue Orient Chrétien* 13 (1908), p. 278.

actions of the solitary. Without this clear acceptance of solitude in its most naked exigencies, the other practices might confuse the issue, or obscure the true end of the solitary life, or even become escapes from it. Once solitude itself is fully accepted, the other practices—fasting, work, vigils, psalmody, and so on gradually fall into place, their need and their efficacy being now properly understood in relation to the whole of "life in the cell." Then asceticism, which at first seems difficult or even impossible, gradually comes to be more easy and even welcome. Each in fact has his own measure and by "sitting in the cell" devoting himself to prayer and the search for God, he will, if he is patient and can accept a certain amount of trial and error in the beginning, finally discover the measure of discipline which he himself requires. The Desert Fathers were quite flexible in this regard, though in principle their asceticism was very severe.

To "sit in the cell" and to "learn from the cell" evidently means first of all learning *that one is not a monk.* That is why the elder in this story did not take the admissions of the disciple too seriously. They showed him, in fact, that the disciple was beginning to learn, and that he was actually opening up to the fruitful lessons of solitude. But in the disciple's own mind, this experience was so defeating and confusing that he could only interpret it in one way: as a sign that he was not called to this kind of life. In fact, in any vocation at all, we must distinguish the grace of the call itself and the preliminary image of ourselves which we spontaneously and almost unconsciously assume to represent the truth of our calling. Sooner or later this image must be destroyed and give place to the concrete reality of the vocation *as lived* in the actual mysterious plan of God, which necessarily contains many elements we could never have foreseen. Thus "sitting in the cell" means learning the fatuity

and hollowness of this illusory image, which was nevertheless necessary from a human point of view and played a
certain part in getting us into the desert.

Another apothegm in the same collection represents a
disciple complaining to an Abba: "My thoughts torment me
saying if you cannot fast or work, at least go and visit the
sick for this also is love." The Elder replies, "Go on, eat,
drink, sleep, only do not leave your cell." (Note that the
Greek words here are interesting—the word for visiting the
sick is *episkopein*, "looking them over as if one were a bishop," we would be inclined to say. The word for leaving the
cell is *apostatein*, with implications for us which we know
well.) The Elder explains: "For the patient bearing of the
cell sets the monk in his right place in the order of things
(*taxis*)."[2]

Afflicted with boredom and hardly knowing what to do
with himself, the disciple represents to himself a more fruitful and familiar way of life, in which he appears to himself
to "be someone" and to have a fully recognizable and acceptable identity, a "place in the Church," but the Elder
tells him that his place in the Church will never be found by
following these ideas and images of a plausible identity.
Rather it is found by travelling a way that is new and disconcerting because it has never been imagined by us before,
or at least we have never conceived it as useful or even
credible for a true Christian—a way in which we seem to
lose our identity and become nothing. Patiently putting up
with the incomprehensible unfulfillment of the lonely, con-
fined, silent, obscure life of the cell, we gradually find our
place, the spot where we belong as monks: that is of course
solitude, the cell itself. This implies a kind of mysterious
awakening to the fact *that where we actually are is where we
belong,* namely in solitude, in the cell. Suddenly we see,
"This is *it.*"

---

2. *Ibid.,* p. 277.

In this particular story, the disciple, driven by sheer boredom, finds some palm leaves, and as if playing around discovers how to split them and weave them together into a basket. Then he teaches himself to wait and not eat until he has finished a certain amount of work, and he fits his "little psalms" into the framework of order that is taking shape and so "by little steps he entered into his order (*taxis*). In so doing, he also gained confidence in his struggle with his inner drives [*logismoi* or thoughts] and overcame them."

With the boredom of the disoriented life comes also *akedia*, or the discouragement, disgust, and lassitude which, says one of the Elders, are the sign and the effect of a certain basic ignorance.[3] Ignorance of what? The old man told the disciple: "You do not have your eye on the *akme* (this has both a temporal and a spatial implication: it is at once the "real point" and the "moment of truth," considered as the "aim" to which we tend in our daily practice) and you do not see the rest that is the object of our hope nor the future punishment" (for failure in this great work). If the disciple only saw all this then even "if your cell were crawling with worms to the point that you were up to your neck in them, you would still bear it patiently without *akedia*."

Another famous saying: "The cell of the hermit is the furnace of Babylon in which the three children found the Son of God and the pillar of cloud in which God spoke to Moses."[4]

St Peter Damian[5] develops this theme rhetorically. In the cell, the hermit fights down the flames of the Babylonian furnace by prayer and faith. There the flames of temptation burn away the bonds by which his limbs are tied without in the least affecting or harming him. The ropes dissolve in fire

---

3. *Ibid.*, p. 277, n. 196.
4. *Ibid.*, p. 279, n. 206.
5. Opusc, XI. c. 19.

and the hermit bursts into a song of praise of the Lord who has freed him: "Dirupisti, Domine, vincula mea" (Ps. 105). For Peter Damian the cell is the fiery kiln in which precious vessels for the King are made. It is a shop in which "happy bargains" (*felix commercium*) are made—earth is traded for heaven. It is the workshop in which the lost likeness of the Creator is reformed in man's soul. The cell itself, says Damian, grants the gift of fasting and of contemplation. "Thou grantest that man may see God with a pure heart, whereas before, wrapped in his own darkness, he did not even know himself." Thus the cell is the place where man comes to know himself first of all that he may know God (Augustine's programme—*Noverim me, noverim Te*). The cell is the sole witness of the divine love flaming in the heart of the monk as he seeks the face of God, says Peter Damian. It is like the Holy Sepulchre, which alone witnessed the resurrection of the Saviour in the night of Easter: the cell is the place of the monk's resurrection to the divine life and light for which he was created and, according to the Irish hermit tradition, the cell will be the place of the hermit's resurrection at the last day. "Whosoever perseveres in his love of thee (O solitary cell) dwells indeed in thee, but God dwells in him."

This is the classic language of contemplative experience. It takes us back to the first saying we quoted, at the beginning of this meditation. To "sit in the cell for the Name of God": this means something at once more concrete and more profound than simply remaining in solitude with the *intention of pleasing God*, or with the holiness of God as a "*sufficient reason*" for one's solitude. At least, we must understand the concept of "sufficient reason" here in great depth. The Name of God is indeed the *ratio* of solitude not only in the sense that "service of God" can be invoked as a plausible explanation for the solitary vocation, but in the sense that in solitude one comes face to face with God himself, present, as the Bible everywhere suggests, "in his Name." The Name of God is the presence of God. The Name of God in the cell is God Himself *as present to the monk* and understood by the monk and understood by the monk as the whole meaning and goal of his vocation. Hence the Name of God is present in the solitude of the cell as the "Son of God" (angel) was present with the children in the fiery furnace and as the pillar of cloud was present to Moses.

Two typical Biblical images here represent *all* the possible Biblical symbols for the inscrutable presence of Yahweh. The Name of God is present in the cell as in the burning bush, in which Yahweh reveals himself as *He who is*. Hence the solitude of the hermit is *engulfed*, so to speak, in the awareness of *QUI EST*. This in fact becomes the true reality of the cell and of solitude, so that the monk who begins by invoking the Name of God to induce him as it were to "come down" to the cell in answer to prayer, gradually comes to realize that the "Name" of God is in fact the heart of the cell, the soul of the solitary life, and that one has been called into solitude not just in order that the Name may be invoked in a certain place, but rather one has been called to meet the Name which is present and waiting in one's own place. It is as though the Name were waiting in the desert for me, and had been preparing this meeting from eternity and in this particular place, this solitude chosen for me. I am called not just to meditate on the Name of God but to encounter God in that Name. Thus the Name becomes, as it were, a cell within a cell, an inner spiritual cell. When I am in the cell or its immediate environs, I should recognize that I am "where the Name of God dwells" and that living in the presence of this great Name I gradually become the one he wills me to be. Thus the life of the cell makes me at once a cell of the Name (which takes deeper and deeper root in my heart) and a dweller in the Name, as if the Name of

God—God himself—were my cell. But since God is infinite, he cannot become a "cell" except in so far as he seems to take on certain limits, in a Name which defines and distinguishes him: as if he were present in his Name and absent elsewhere. (Yet at the same time he is in all, through all things.) But it is from the vantage point of the particular solitude in which I meet and discover his Name for myself that I can understand his presence everywhere else. Thus the reason for stability in solitude is that the hermit goes wandering out of solitude in the world; the "presence" of God may remain as an abstraction which he knows but which he no longer experiences in all the concreteness that is demanded and that is possible when the Name is present in the cell. True, of course, the Name goes with me wherever I invoke him, and dwells in my heart everywhere, but this is thanks to the cell. Here we see the Name implies not only identity but WILL and LOVE. The name that overshadows the monk in the cloud of solitude is the creative and redemptive will of our Father, and this Name impregnates everything with a redemptive and loving significance, with promises of love and salvation, with invitations to compassion and intercession for all men. Thus through the Name of God the solitary comes to the knowledge of him who makes himself present in solitude.

Above all, of course, he reveals his Name as that of JESUS, Saviour, in whom and with whom I am one with all men. Thus my place as intercessor and brother is also my solitude and my cell where I find and love all men in the warm and human love of the presence of Christ, for it is the Word Incarnate (signified by the pillar of cloud and by the angel present in the furnace) who alone can give me full comfort in trials that are essentially human and bound up with my physical being. There is no peace and no reality in an abstract, discarnate, gnostic solitude. St Peter Damian insists that since the Christian hermit is hidden in Jesus

Christ he is therefore most intimately present (*praesentissimus*) to all the rest of the Church. His isolation in solitude unites him more closely in love with all the rest of his brothers in the world. Hence there is every good reason for the hermit to say *Dominus vobiscum* in his office and Mass even though no one may be physically present. We can see here the implications of having the Blessed Sacrament reserved in the hermit's cell.

The mercy, the compassion, the human-hearted wise and ever faithful love of God (all these are Names in the Name) are represented in a new and surprising, but very tender form in one of the apothegms.[6] A brother asks one of the old men what he should do if in affliction and loneliness he should be left helpless with no one to whom he might explain his trouble. The answer is that God will send help "if you pray in truth," and this is illustrated by a story. At Scete a hermit was suffering in absolute isolation with no one to console or help him in any way. He got his things together in order to leave the desert. "Then divine grace appeared to him in the form of a virgin who encouraged him and said: Do not go away BUT STAY HERE WITH ME, for none of the evils you have imagined has ever happened to you. HE OBEYED AND STAYED THERE, and at this moment his heart was healed."

Here is a deep and moving insight into the reality of that Name which is also full of tenderness and which is revealed as Wisdom, Sophia, and in whose mysterious and beautiful form God is pleased to make himself present to the children of men (Prov. 8:1).

The Book of Wisdom speaks of this mysterious and intimate love of man for divine wisdom as his bride and friend whom he has preferred to everything else. "For all the gold in the world, compared with her, is but a little sand and

---

6. Nau, *op. cit.*, p. 283, n. 215.

next to her all silver counts as mud" (Wis. 7:9). "But with her friendship one becomes truly the friend of God" (Wis. 7:14). "She makes them friends of God and prophets, for God loves only those who dwell with wisdom" (Wis. 7:27-8).

This then is the true secret of the cell, a paradise in which he who is called meets, in silence, awareness and peace the consoling and healing presence of that wisdom whose beauty is "a reflection of the eternal light and a spotless mirror of the doings of God, the image of his excellence" (Wis. 7:26).

> For she is fairer than the sun
> > and surpasses every constellation of the stars.
> Compared to light, she takes precedence;
> > for that, indeed, night supplants,
> > but wickedness prevails not over Wisdom.
> Indeed, she reaches from end to end mightily
> > and governs all things well.
> Her I loved and sought after from my youth;
> > I sought to take her for my bride
> > and was enamoured of her beauty.
> > > (Wis. 7:29 - 8:2)

Feast of St Benedict, 1966

THE CASE FOR A RENEWAL OF EREMITISM
IN THE MONASTIC STATE

The Case for a Renewal of Eremitism in the Monastic State

Would we be yielding to an exaggerated idealism if we were to hope for a decisive renewal of the hermit life in the bosom of the Western Church? We may judge, on the contrary, that God could give the world no more persuasive sign of the persistent, untiring action of his Spirit among men.

— Théophile Reclus, in *La Vie Spirituelle*, October 1952, p. 242.

To glorify eremitism in general seems to me to be a dangerous thing, for each vocation to solitude is a problem of spiritual direction and aspirants should not be encouraged, without distinction, to seek it.

— S., in *La Vie Spirituelle*, October 1952, p. 278.

I

The time has come for a renewal of the eremitical life within the monastic state. There are monastic Orders which still strive to maintain a semi-eremitical life, as the basis of their observance. But the traditional comprehension of the purely solitary life as a normal fulfillment of the monastic vocation in certain cases, within the framework of monasticism itself, needs to be rediscovered.

There still exists a traditional distinction in the Western Church between the eremitical state and the religious state, even though there is nothing explicit in the present Code of

Canon Law [*i.e.*, the 1917 Code: see Canon 603 of the 1983 Code—*ed.*] about hermits. Yet the distinction is affirmed implicitly in Canon 487: "Status religiosus seu stabilis *in communi* vivendi modus . . ." The Code of the Oriental Church includes the hermits in the monastic state, and does not consider them outside that state at all (see Canon 313). It would be worth while to study in detail just how this Western distinction came into being, but such a study must be left for another occasion. The materials are abundant but there is much work to be done in organizing and interpreting the various data. It must suffice to indicate, very briefly, how the distinction arose, and this will situate our remarks on the eremitical renewal in their proper historical and canonical context, since we are here concerned not with the eremitical state as apart from the religious state, but with the possibility of a renewal of eremitism within the religious state itself. We might remark at the outset that a monk living as hermit near his monastery would not necessarily cease to participate both spiritually and materially in the "common life" in the sense of Canon 487. Indeed he would be much more of a participant in the common life of his monastery than a monk serving as pastor in a parish a thousand miles away, who barely, if ever, returns to his community.

As is well known, the present renewal of eremitism which is associated with Dom Jacques Winandy and the Hermits of St John Baptist in British Columbia is taking the form of a *pia unio* and hence is going on outside the religious state, even though most of the hermits have come from Benedictine or Cistercian monasteries, and remain members of their Orders. The "eremitical state" in this sense is closer to the lay state than to the status of religious or of monk, since the hermit outside the religious state is not vowed to poverty. The hermits properly so called, according to this definition, are proprietors without vows. It may be mentioned that the very interesting article of Dom P. Doyère on "Ermites" in the *Dictionnaire de Droit Canonique* is concerned chiefly with hermits in this sense, though he does devote some space to eremitism in the religious state.

Writing in the *Vie Spirituelle, Supplément*,[1] Dom Winandy pleaded for a recognition of the hermit state as canonically distinct from the religious state. Even though he admitted that hermit vocations were arising particularly in Monastic Orders (he cited the cases of five priests in the Congregation of Solesmes who had received *Exclaustrationes ad Nutum Sanctae Sedis* to become hermits), he felt that the most satisfactory solution was exclaustration and therefore departure from the religious state. He took into account the serious ambiguities this would imply, since actually exclaustration has a certain note of ignominy about it—a "step down," which is disconcerting canonically, just when the hermit is presumably taking a "step up" spiritually. But unfortunately, as Dom Doyère's article shows, the hermit state as it was canonically constituted in the late Middle Ages is in fact a "step down" from the monastic state. However this "step down" could be accepted as a motive for greater poverty and humility: "L'état érémitique présente un caractère *mineur*, un caractère d'humilité et de complet effacement."[2] We shall return to Dom Winandy's article, which is the most important contemporary treatment of our question so far.

Originally the hermit life was considered to be the normal perfection of the monastic life. The hermit was then the monk *par excellence*. The cenobitic life, even when not actually oriented to eremitism as its fulfillment, participated to a great extent, by silence, enclosure, etc., in the solitary character of the hermit vocation.

We need not dwell here on some of the extraordinary

---

1. *La Vie Spirituelle, Supplément*, vol. XII (1959), pp. 343ff.
2. *D.D.C.*, 5, p. 418.

charisms of the solitary life found in the records of Syrian and Egyptian monachism from the fourth to the seventh centuries. The spread of the monastic ideal to the West, aided as it was by the diffusion of St Athanasius' *Vita Antonii* in the mid-fourth century, was marked by an emphasis on eremitism. The eremitical and cenobitic ideals developed harmoniously together in the monasticism of St Martin in west-central Gaul and in that of Cassian and Honoratus in the south-east, not to mention the monks of the Alps and the Jura.

Already in the fifth century we find a council in Gaul legislating for hermits. The Council of Vannes in 463 provides as follows:

> *Servandum quoque de monachis ne eis ad solitarias cellulas liceat a congregatione discedere nisi forte probatis post emeritos labores aut propter infirmitatis necessitatem ab abbatibus regula remittatur. Quod ita demum fiet ut intra eadem monasterii septa manentes, tamen sub abbatis potestate separatas habere cellulas permittantur.*[8]

This text is concerned exclusively with the passage from the cenobitic to the solitary life within the unified monastic state, while remaining a member of one's community and subject to one's own abbot. The following points may be noted:

1. In common with most of the early legislation, the point at issue is to regulate the transition from community to solitude and to limit it to those who have a serious reason for making the change and who are well prepared to do so. See also Council of Agde (506), Canon 38; Council of Orleans (543), Canon 23; Toledo (633), Canon 53; Toledo (646), Canon 5; Frankfurt (794), Canon 12, etc. The Council in Trullo (692) concerns itself with requirements

---

3. Mansi, 7, 954. Text quoted from H. Leclercq, "Reclus," in *D.A.C.L.*, 14, 2149-59.

for reclusion: it demands three years of cenobitic life and one year of solitary life as pre-requisites for this most exacting form of solitary life.[4]

2. In particular, insistence is placed on the fact that the solitary must be one who has been proved and tested by *emeritos labores* in the cenobitic community. He must prove himself a monk, for if he is not yet a worthy monk in the *cenobium*, he will hardly be any better in solitude. This same question is repeatedly taken up in the Councils of the fifth to seventh centuries, and it provides the background for the familiar, one might say classic, text in Chapter One of the Benedictine Rule: "*Qui non conversionis fervore novitio sed Monasterii probatione diuturna didicerunt contra diabolum multorum solatio iam docti pugnare . . .* etc." ("[Then, the second kind are anchorites or hermits, who have progressed beyond the first fervour of monastic life. They] have been tested for a long time in the monastery and have learned from their companionship with many others how to fight against the devil"—trans. D. Catherine Wybourne, O.S.B. [*ed.*]). In short, the eremitical life is considered a normal fulfillment of the monastic life, but it must not be embraced prematurely and without the control of obedience.

3. At the same time the Council of Vannes permits a monk to live in a solitary cell for another reason: bodily or perhaps mental illness, *propter infirmitatis necessitatem.*

4. Care is to be taken in either case that this solitary cell is within the monastic enclosure and that the solitary, whether hermit or merely invalid, remains under obedience to his abbot. The prescription that the hermit should be within the enclosure appears to have been broadly interpreted.

5. In any event, we have here what seems to be regarded as the normal situation. It is considered perfectly normal to make provision for a certain exceptional solitude within the framework of the monastic life. The hermit monk is to be

---

4. Dom Besse, in *D.T.C.*, 1, 1139.

protected by enclosure and obedience. But is it enough to call this "eremitism?" There is a further distinction between the hermit and the recluse. Gregory of Tours and many other early writers, especially hagiographers and chroniclers, bear witness to the frequency of *reclusion* as the pefect form of solitary life that is specifically germane to the monastic *institution*. The recluse, enclosed in a cell, is completely dependent on others for physical and spiritual care. This certainly implies "community." Hence the cell of the recluse (or "anchorage") will normally adjoin a church, perhaps a monastic church. Saint-Gall is an example of an abbey where reclusion was held in honour. The area of Metz, Trier and Liège was rich in recluses. The Rule for Recluses (*Regula Solitariorum*) by Grimlaicus (ninth century) was evidently written by a priest-recluse of Metz. This Rule for Recluses had more influence than is generally supposed. A recent article has shown that it became the basis for the observance of reclusion in the Camaldolese hermitages, where reclusion is still held to be a further perfection of the eremitical-monastic life.[5] A study of Grimlaicus and the very nature of reclusion itself suggests that in the High Middle Ages reclusion was a normal form of solitude for the cenobite who, in his anchorage, continued visibly to be a special part of the community, already "entombed" in a life of eschatological contemplation, and perhaps exercising a charismatic apostolate in his "prison."

The High Middle Ages were years of formation and of crisis in western monasticism. St Benedict already speaks of the problem of the wandering monk. After the Viking invasions swept the Celtic monks and hermits from the Hebrides, Orkneys, and other islands where they had gone to find "a desert in the sea," the Irish, who were already fond of pilgrimages, descended in even greater numbers upon the

---

5. J. Cacciamani, "La Réclusion dans l'Ordre Camaldule," *R.A.M.* (1962), pp. 142, 15l.

continent. Irish monasteries grew up on the continent, as at Corbie and Peronne. Later we see the famous Schotten-kloster in Regensburg and other Bavarian cities. Reclusion was of course in favour with them. For various reasons, including the fact that many of the wandering monks were also, incidentally, bishops (*episcopi vagi*) without a diocese, the pilgrim-eremitism of the Celts may have aggravated a problem that had been regarded as very disturbing particularly since the Carolingian reform. This fact may have contributed to the sense that hermits needed to be regulated, and certainly the "crisis of cenobitism" in the twelfth century brought up once again this same aspect of the problem.[6]

Meanwhile, it might be of interest to refresh our memory on the Irish question in the High Middle Ages. It has been said of the Celtic wanderers:

> The appearance of the strangers must have been striking. They had long flowing hair and tattooed certain parts of the body, especially the eyelids. Their tonsure went from ear to ear, that is to say the front part of the scalp only was shaved. . . . Their love of wandering was proverbial. . . . The famous scholar Dungal wrote that the Franks disliked his countrymen because of their noisy clamour. . . .[7]

Dungal was himself a recluse at Saint-Denis.

A certain spirit of independence and the attachment to strange customs must have made the Celts seem something of a problem on the Continent. But there were also other pilgrims (the Anglo-Saxons especially) on the road. Besides that, Oriental visitors, Greek and Syrian monks, brought their own customs and religious ways to the West, and we find references to monasteries of Greek and Irish monks living together celebrating their own liturgies side by side.

---

6. See for instance G. Morin, "Rainaud l'ermite et Ives de Chartres," in *R.B* (1928), 101ff.
7. J. M. Clark, *The Abbey of St. Gall as a Centre of Literature and Art* (Cambridge, 1926), p. 27

It must not be imagined that these problems of order arose exclusively from a lack of legislation and from a too-free development of "charisms" of pilgrimage, hermit-solitude or reclusion. On the contrary, it was precisely the influence of canonical and penitential measures that aggravated the problem of the wandering monk and indeed of the wandering Christian in the High Middle Ages. The common Irish practice of sending monks into exile or on pilgrimage for sins, or indeed for simple irregularities, and the equally common practice of sending sinners and criminals on pilgrimage resulted in mixed bands of monastic and lay penitents travelling about to fulfill canonical penances. The result was disastrous.

We might here briefly summarize the ways in which the problem of organizing and regulating eremitism was met in the time of the Gregorian reform and after. Most of the solutions were within the monastic state.

1. First of all the Church blessed and encouraged the formation of well-organized communities of hermits dwelling in *lauras*, as at Camaldoli or Fonte Avellana. This led eventually to the establishment of "Orders" such as the Camaldolese, the Carthusians, the Grandmontines (or *Bons Hommes*), etc. It may be mentioned here that Congregations such as the "Hermits of St Augustine"ceased to be in any sense eremitical almost as soon as they were formed.

2. Reclusion of a monk belonging to a cenobitic house (or to a *laura* of hermits) remained in principle the traditional solution for the member of a *cenobium* who wanted a more perfect solitude without leaving his monastery. This practice was more common in some areas than in others. It is found in certain English abbeys (*e.g.* Westminster) all through the Middle Ages. Speaking, of the Westminster recluses, Dom David Knowles says:

> Here at the heart of what must always have been one of the most distracted and least secluded of communities,

> provision was made for a recluse who had been and indeed still was a monk of the house. . . . This may have been regarded as an attempt to implement a commonly neglected passage in the Rule of St Benedict [he refers to the passage on anchorites in Chapter One].[8]

Knowles adds that it is not clear whether the recluses at Durham, Sherborne, Worcester, etc. were monks of the community. On the whole the recluses ("ancres") tended to be women rather than men. There grew up a rather widespread practice of reclusion of women in cells adjoining parish and other churches. Often anchorages were benefices at the disposition of the Abbot of a monastery. Saint Albans, in England, was especially active in patronizing recluses (for instance Christina of Markyate). Nevertheless these women were very frequently associated with monastic communities, at least spiritually. They received the habit of the Cistercians or Benedictines, they followed modified monastic rules, and so on.

Saint Albans was one of the big Benedictine Abbeys of the Middle Ages which, like Cluny, Montserrat, Subiaco, Lérins, Marmoutier, and the like permitted and even encouraged some of its monks to become hermits, while remaining under obedience to their abbot. Temporary as well as permanent retirement into solitude was common. Often cenobites would obtain permission to spend Lent in a hermitage, or to make more or less long retreats apart from the community, and Dom Henri Leclercq said: "Few are the saints who have not spent more or less time in solitude."[9] These hermitages were sometimes close to the monastery, sometimes far from it, but generally on monastery property. There are numerous references which take for granted those *fratres qui solent sedere longius a monasterio*. They are treated with love and respect and the brethren are glad to see them

---

8. *Religious Orders in England,* 2, p. 219.
9. *D.A.C.L,* "Reclus," p. 2150.

when they occasionally visit the monastery for the synaxis and assist at the sermon in chapter. They are praised for the humility and charity they show in visiting the community, and the brethren are not to rebuke them for doing so.[10] In the twelfth century there was a group of at least six monks of Saint Albans living several miles from the monastery in the hills, with one of them acting as their spiritual Father. However, it was also possible for a monk simply to sever his bonds with his monastic community in order to embrace the hermit life, perhaps, even in a distant country.

3. Eremitism thus developed outside the juridical framework of monasticism, and once again England was especially rich in non-monastic hermits of this type, who produced an eremitical literature of high quality that permanently influenced the tradition of English spirituality. We need only mention the poet and mystic Richard Rolle. On one hand there were small loosely organized congregations of hermits, who made vows before the Bishop, and on the other there were non-monastic hermits without vows making their own living and owning their own little plot of land, or receiving a hermitage as a benefice or cure, who came to form a perfectly distinct state, and they were watched over by the bishops. Gradually they formed a class apart, made up of simple and often illiterate or eccentric personages who nevertheless lived devout and useful lives as bridge-keepers, road-menders, lighthouse-keepers, or custodians of remote chapels and places of pilgrimage.

4. Finally, under the inspiration of St Francis, the mendicant Orders favoured the solitary trend in their own milieu. There is a lively and rich Franciscan tradition of eremitism, developing into the *ritiro* movement of later centuries. The Franciscan *ritiro* is analogous to the Carmelite "desert" (instituted in the sixteenth century) as a small, solitary and poor community where eremitism or very simple and primi-

---

10. See Dom J. Leclercq, *Studia Anselmiana* 40 (1956), 105.

tive cenobitism can be practiced either temporarily for a few months, for a year or two, or for life. The Dominicans, incidentally, generally seem to have sought their greater solitude as recluses, when they did not transfer to the ancient eremitical Orders. It would be interesting to keep these other solutions in mind as we proceed in our study, but unfortunately space does not permit us to consider the mendicant Orders. We will confine ourselves to *monastic* hermits.

5. Another solution was that of the Cistercians, who officially showed disfavour to eremitism, but encouraged a very simple and remote form of community life in which isolation and silence were explicitly supposed to provide an ambience of solitude in which the monastic ideal could be realized without resort to eremitism or reclusion. Twelfth-century Benedictines in northern England who wanted a more austere life would at times transfer to the Cistercians or at times repair to hermitages belonging to their own monastery—such as the hermitage on Farne Island in the North Sea, occupied by monks from Durham. From this it will be seen that the austerity and silence of the twelfth-century Cistercians made them rank with hermits in the eyes of the broader and more active cenobitic communities. The Cistercians seem to have been proud of the fact that they attracted hermits to their monasteries, as this seemed to indicate that the Cistercian life was a higher and more perfect way than that of the hermit. Hence the practice of investing hermits with the Cistercian habit and then including them in the Menology and even in the liturgical calendar (St Galgan, for example, was solemnly invested with the habit *after death*). In practice there were also a few Cistercian hermits, as we shall see. However it appears that the Cistercian Order preferred its members to leave the Order entirely if they intended to be hermits (see below).

II

Having thus outlined the historical background against which we must consider the question of a renewal of hermit life within the monastic state today, we might also draw attention briefly to some of the material that might be studied more thoroughly in order to discover principles and norms to help us in understanding such a renewal.

The question of vocation: Obviously the most important question of all is that of determining the vocation of a monk who claims to be called to the solitary life. Is such a vocation possible? Is it normal?

Following St Bernard, Cistercians have so consistently answered "No" to this question that we have come to regard an exclusively cenobitic monasticism as the sole norm. The monastic life is a common life and sets a standard by which everything else, even an exceptional and modified eremitism in connection with a *cenobium*, is to be regarded with extreme distrust as a hazardous and perhaps delusive adventure. Dom Jean Leclercq reminds us:

> We have developed the habit of regarding eremitism in reference to cenobitism considered as "normal" monasticism which provides the norm for everybody. . . . This was not the traditional attitude.[11]

As a result of this wrong attitude, with the common life regarded as the *ne plus ultra*, the plea of the hermit vocation is dismissed as a delusion prompted by a spirit of independence and instability. And in some cases it may well be so. The point is, however, that this empirical fact must not be made into a general abstract principle which admits of no exceptions whatever.

In the Cistercian golden age, St Aelred stands out among many others as a witness to the traditional respect for soli-

---

11. J. Leclercq, "L'érémitisme en Occident jusqu'a l'an mil," in *Le Millénaire du Mont Athos* (Chevetogne, 1963), p. 178.

tude. A glance at his tract on the life of reclusion, written for his sister, shows that he readily admits that some people have a special need for solitude. Because of this, Aelred accepts without question the ancient tradition of eremitism or reclusion. "For some people," says Aelred, "it is actually harmful to live among many companions (*inter multos vivere perniciosum*). For others it is at least an impediment, and for some who can live with 'many others' without difficulty, it may still be more fruitful to dwell in greater retirement: (*secretius habitare magis aestimant fructuosum*)." Aelred is speaking in altogether general terms, and hence there is no logical exclusion of Cistercian monks from his categories. As a matter of fact we shall see that Revesby, an abbey of which Aelred was founder and first abbot, had three hermitages, at least one of which probably dated back to his time. He admits without too much difficulty that the sincere and well-considered conviction of the one "called" to solitude is something that can be accepted within the bounds of ordinary prudence. The fact that such persons themselves believe (*magis aestimant*) that a more hidden life would be more fruitful for them is not, therefore, to be taken as a delusion until proved otherwise, but rather as a reasonable and good spiritual option until shown to be otherwise. However, because of the danger of a too-free and unstable form of eremitism, the strict life of reclusion is accepted by Aelred as a higher and safer way of life than that of the simple hermit.[12] In any case, Aelred is by no means blind to the dangers and abuses found in the anchorages of his time. He describes them, not without rhetorical amplification.

William of Saint-Thierry left us a classic eulogy of the solitary life in the opening chapter of his *Golden Epistle*, where he praises the rebirth of that *orientale lumen*, that

---

12. *De Institutione Inclusarum*, Pt. 1, n. 2. See C. Dumont, trans., *La Vie de Recluse* (Sources Chrétiennes 76) (Paris, 1961), pp. 43ff.

caelestis forma conversationis, that *antiqua vitae solitariae gloria* in the forest of the Ardennes. He multiplies the familiar tropes on the dignity of the solitary vocation and adds: *Sileant ergo qui in tenebris de luce judicantes vos arguunt novitatis ex abundantia malae voluntatis: ipsi potius arguendi vetustatis et vanitatis.*[13] He is speaking of Carthusians, and here even St Bernard would agree with him. But there is no doubt that for William eremitism has an essential part in the *ordo monasticus*.

The fourth Advent Sermon of Guerric of Igny praises the desert life, consecrated by the fast of Jesus, and speaks of the Cistercian monasteries as deserts where the monk is alone in silence, but has the support of *sancta societas* with his silent brethren.[14] Here it must be admitted that Guerric is praising the eremitical spirit rather than the actual practice of physical solitude. But the eremitical spirit cannot be kept alive without concrete examples of lives lived alone with God.

The letters of St Peter Damian provide us with interesting material on the eremitical vocation and on particular canonical problems that arose within his eremitical reform. St Peter Damian is consistently opposed to the opulence and relative comfort of the big cenobitic communities of the eleventh century. He emphatically prefers the hermit life and encourages passage from the *cenobium* to the hermit life as a normal progress in the perfection of the monk. When a monk has embraced the solitary life, he must remain stable in it, and regard all thought of return to the *cenobium* as a temptation to be manfully resisted. He writes with strong disapproval when his nephew Damian, a hermit, is persuaded to go back to the monastery to follow a course in sacred chant (*pro discendis ecclesiasticae cantilena modulis*).[15] "When I heard this," says the saint, "it seemed to me that I had

---

13. Lib. I, C 1, *P.L.*, 184, 310-11.
14. *P.L.*, 185, 22.
15. *Epist.* VI. 22. *P.L.*, 144, 405.

been told of a frail lamb wandering forth from the sheep fold into the bloody jaws of the ravening wolf." The young monk must therefore return to the hermitage in all haste.

Needless to say that Peter Damian joined the other reformers of his time in condemning wandering hermits, whether they were merely making pilgrimage a pretext for instability, or whether they claimed to have a charism of preaching and prophecy.[16]

It can be said that St Peter Damian disapproved of eremitism outside the monastic state as much as he approved of the monk-hermits who remained in the established or renewed monastic institutions.

Dom Leclercq has published a letter in which St Peter Damian approves the petition of two hermits who do not want to go down to the *cenobium* even when they are ill (they may stay in the hermitage, he says, as long as they do not have to eat meat). They have asked to be buried in the hermitage (not in the cemetery of the *cenobium*), and he approves this also as a sign of stability.[17]

St Peter Damian admits postulants directly to the hermitage without previous training in the *cenobium*, which, he implies, may in some cases be undesirable.[18] In any event, he foresees that newcomers can be gradually accustomed to the rigours of the hermit life. An interesting chapter of the same Opuscule[19] gives some motives for leaving the *cenobium* in order to be a hermit. St Peter Damian thinks that the cenobite who is a prospective hermit ought to give some thought to the disadvantages of the *cenobium*: *superstitiosas quasdam monasticae disciplinae censuras, supervacuos tintinnabulorum clangores, cantilenarum multiplices harmonisa, ornamentorum phaleras . . .*[20] The complexity and in some sense the "vani-

---

16. See St Peter Damian, *Opusculum* XII, ch. 24, *P.L.*, 145, 277.
17. *Studia Anselmiana* 18 (1947), pp. 283-93.
18. Opusc. XV, 29, *P.L.*, 145, 361.
19. Opusc. XV, 30, *P.L.*, 145, 362.
20. *Loc. cit.*

ty" of an observance that St Peter Damian does not shrink from calling superstitious contrasts unfavourably in his mind with the simple austerity and freedom of spirit that should be the hallmark of the hermit life. He quotes St Paul to this effect, and the prospective hermit is to be persuaded that he will serve God much better in the simplicity and freedom of the hermitage. Nevertheless, the advantages of the *cenobium* must also be remembered, and if the young hermit starts getting too complacent, emphasis must be placed on obedience and humility, cenobitic virtues which, in the hermitages of St Peter Damian, form an essential part of the solitary life, but which would normally be best learned in the *cenobium*.

St Peter Damian makes no difficulty about admitting that not all hermits are blessed with humility and a pure intention. Many have failed to take advantage of cenobitic obedience to form their spirit. Opuscule 51 gives a diverting portrait of a cenobite who, after insulting his abbot, has marched off into solitude under the prompting of his own self-will and who, when Peter and the Abbot came to visit him, thrusts them unceremoniously out, heaping them with choice insults. The trouble with this hermit, says St Peter Damian, is that he has never been properly formed in humility. He has learned to show off his austerity in an urban monastery. He has become self-willed and singular. He is argumentative and stubborn, and accepts no authoritative statement about anything. When the example of the saints is proposed to him, including that of St Romuald himself, this hermit dismisses it with a wave of the hand: "How do I know they were saints anyway?" Even in this case, however, St Peter does not advise him to return to the *cenobium*, but tries to inculcate a little humility and patience into the man, so that he may become a true hermit and live worthily in solitude.

While St Bernard had the greatest admiration for the

Carthusians and for certain hermits like the Jezelinus who was living naked in the woods of Luxembourg, and while Bernard commended himself to the prayers of holy solitaries and recluses living in the Holy Land,[21] he nevertheless emphatically and habitually discouraged passage from the *cenobium* to eremitical solitude. A typical letter of St Bernard on this subject has been published by Dom Leclercq. It is addressed to a Cistercian (probably English) who has repeatedly sought St Bernard's approval for his "hermit vocation." Bernard calls it an imprudent desire and refuses to countenance it. Though he does not attack the hermit vocation as such, he seems to think that the desire for solitude is usually a deception. *Solent enim hujusmodi desideria de Spiritu concepi levitatis, ab hiis praesertim qui vires suas metiri nescientes, indiscrete affectant quae eis non expedit.*[22] And he proposes a general principle: not to leave what is certain for what is uncertain. St Bernard concludes by invoking his own apostolic authority in order to command the monk to remain where he is. It is curious that another Cistercian uses this identical principle to solve a "case" in moral theology: that of a hermit who has a vow to remain in solitude and who is asked to leave his cell and undertake apostolic work. Guy de l'Aumône, a Cistercian abbot and theologian of the thirteenth century, resolves the case by this principle: *tenendum eat certum et dimittendum incertum.* The hermit therefore should remain in solitude where he belongs.[23]

There is an interesting letter attributed to St Bernard and found in a manuscript volume in the collection of the Abbey of Gethsemani. It has recently been published by Dom Jean Leclercq.[24] Far from condemning the solitary life, this letter is a traditional eulogy of "the cell" and "the desert,"

---

21. See Letter 288. *P.L.*, 182, 494c.
22. *Analecta S.O.C.* IX (1953), 138.
23. *Studia Monastica*, IV, I (1962), p. 101.
24. *Studia Monastica*, IV, I (1962), pp. 937ff.

and contains copious quotations from St Peter Damian's praise of the hermit life. Commenting on this letter Dom Leclercq treats it as another indication that the early Cistercians were closely related to the eremitical movement in monastic reform, and says "this letter bears witness to the favour which the eremitical idea often enjoyed in the past in Cistercian *milieux*."[25] Other texts of St Bernard (authentic) have found their way into collections "on the hermit life" and the fact that this letter is attributed to him at least shows that such an attribution was looked upon as credible in the fifteenth century when the manuscript was written. Thus we must not insist, without further qualification, that Bernard was always and unchangingly opposed to eremitical vocation. In point of fact, the formula "*O beata solitudo, o sola beatitudo*" was attributed to St Bernard. The letter in the Gethsemani manuscript contains the phrase "*O solitudo beata.*" The letter purports to be one of advice to a new hermit who has "recently entered upon the holy warfare" (of the solitary life). The cell is praised as the paradise where Christ dwells with the monk. Peace is found in the cell, outside there is nothing but conflict. The silence of the desert is the source of wisdom, and this wisdom is developed above all by meditation in solitude upon the mysteries of Christ. It is quite likely that this letter is the product of some Cistercian *milieu*, probably one in which there were recluses. South Germany naturally suggests itself. While not regarding the attribution to St Bernard as totally implausible, Dom Leclercq does not seem to take it very seriously. But this letter was very probably written by a Cistercian to another Cistercian who had just embraced the solitary life as a recluse.

However, there is one Cistercian hermit who was without question closely associated with St Bernard and who is said to have gone to Palestine with Bernard's blessing to live

---

25. *Loc. cit*, p. 94

there as a solitary. This is Blessed Conrad, for whom there is a feast in the Cistercian calendar on 14 February. The facts about his hermit vocation are very obscure and uncertain, but it is possible that Conrad was a monk who had passed from Clairvaux to Morimond and who had departed irregularly from Morimond in the company of Abbot Arnold, in a notorious scandal which would presumably not dispose St Bernard too well toward projects for foundations in Palestine. Nevertheless it is still held to be certain that Conrad went to live as a hermit in the east with St Bernard's approval.[26]

Whatever may have been St Bernard's feelings about the hermit life, and whatever may have been the weight of his authority in the matter, we must remember the forceful statement made by "Apostolus" (*i.e.* M. D. Chenu), writing in the special number of *La Vie Spirituelle* on solitude: "It is for the Church to discern and to test the spirits, but she cannot bring it about that one who is truly called by the Spirit to holy solitude, is not in fact called."[27]

In practice the Cistercian Order did admit the possibility of a monk becoming a hermit on the property of his monastery, and among the saints of the Order the most outstanding example of this is St Albert of Sestri, a lay brother of St Andrew's monastery in Liguria (Italy) who received his abbot's permission to live a solitary, penitent life in a hut in the nearby forest. He spent thirty years there, working miracles and dying in the odour of sanctity in 1239.[28] His cult was approved by Innocent IV. The lives of the saints of the Order would reveal not a few examples of relative or temporary solitude, and the brothers dwelling in granges sometimes found that this more lonely life contributed to their

---

26. See J. Grillon, "Saint Bernard et les ermites," in *Bernard de Clairvaux* (Paris, 1953, p. 253).
27. *La Vie Spirituelle* 377 (October 1952), p. 299.
28. *Hagiologium Cist.* 46, vol. 1, pp. 144-5.

sanctification. However, many "hermit saints" in the annals of the Order were men who renounced eremitical solitude to become Cistercians and afterward departed again into solitude or on pilgrimage (*e.g.* Bd Famianus).

In any case the validity of vocation to the solitary life has clearly been admitted in practice within the Cistercian Order as well as anywhere else. We possess for example a letter of Stephen of Lexington, apostolic visitor of the Irish monasteries of white monks in the thirteenth century, in which he takes up the question, and permits two monks and a brother of Holy Cross Abbey to become hermits.[29] He recognizes that they have had a long-standing attraction to the solitary life "but that they did not dare to put this desire into effect because they believed that such aspirations could not be carried out by Cistercians without the counsel of the General Chapter." However, they have applied to his special apostolic authority and in virtue of this he grants their petition. It is interesting to note in what terms he does so. He frees them from their bond of obedience to the Order, and puts them under the full jurisdiction of the bishop in whose diocese they intend to settle. If they do not live worthily as hermits, then the bishop must deprive them of their Cistercian habit and punish them in other suitable ways. Here we have an instance of what may have been considered the "best solution" for Cistercians desiring to be hermits in the Middle Ages: the change of life also involves a change of state. In order to become a hermit one ceases juridically to be a monk; one passes from obedience to one's abbot to obedience under a bishop. The monastic habit is still worn, but one is now in a different state of life, that of the hermit. If this was what "becoming a hermit" meant in the Cistercian context, we can readily understand St Bernard's objections. On the other hand, we can assume that

---

29. Letter XX in *Registrum Epistolarum Stephani*, ed. B. Griesser, *Analecta S.O.C.* (1946), p. 27.

those monks who retired to a hermitage or anchorage belonging to their own monastery or to some other monastery probably did not leave the monastic state.

Canonically the letter of Stephen of Lexington is perhaps the most interesting document on this subject that has come down to us from the early centuries of the Cistercian Order. It is not clear from this letter whether or not Stephen of Lexington is assenting to the proposition that petitions to embrace the hermit life normally had to be approved by the General Chapter. This is a point that merits further study.

III

We may now briefly consider the evidence offered by monastic history to show that in actual fact hermitages and anchorages depending on Cistercian and Benedictine monasteries were quite plentiful in the Middle Ages. We have already mentioned such famous cases as Westminster, Saint Albans and Durham. Another typical case is that of Cluny. Some of the monks who were venerated after their death as saints of Cluny were, in fact, hermits: for instance Bd Adhegrinus who, in the tenth century, first made a three-year trial of the solitary life and then established himself permanently in a hermitage two miles from the monastery, where he lived as a quasi-recluse (*parva spelunca subarctus*), but came down to the monastery for Sundays and big Feasts.[30]

Another monk of Cluny, Anastasius, first obtained permission from Peter the Venerable to spend his Lents in solitude. He later got permission to retire as a hermit into the Pyrenees, where he established himself on a high mountain. Later he was called back to visit his brethren, but died on the way to Cluny.[31] St Hugh of Cluny allowed two

---

30. See J. Leclercq, "Pierre le Vénérable et l'érémitisme clunisien," *Studia Anselmiana* 40, pp. 106-7.
31. *Op cit.*, pp 107-8.

monks to live as hermits on the Atlantic coast in the diocese of Bordeaux, where later a small community of monk-hermits acted as lighthouse keepers.[32] Peter the Venerable allowed one of his secretaries to live as a hermit for a while, but later called him back because he needed his help.[33] For the monk Gerard of Cluny, who lived apart from the monastery on a lonely wooded hill with several other like-minded companions, Peter the Venerable wrote a letter which can be classed as a "Rule" for monastic hermits.[34]

It is interesting to note that various degrees of partial solitude were also encouraged at Cluny. There was a quiet part of the church set aside for those who preferred solitary contemplative prayer. It was possible to withdraw for a time of retreat to hermitages near the monastery. One monk was allowed to have a cell in a high tower where he could retire to meditate and pray. Reclusion also existed within the framework of the common life at Cluny. Here again we see that the spirit of Cluny differs from that of Cîteaux. The Cistercian hermit often had to cut himself off forever from his Order. The Cluniac on the contrary, even though he might be living as a hermit hundreds of miles from his monastic home, was normally considered a member of the family and could even be summoned back for no other purpose than to visit the brethren and spend a little time with them.

There is a great deal of material about Cistercian recluses, but unfortunately it is not always clear that they were monks or nuns of the Order who had received permission to become recluses. More often they appear to have been holy men or especially holy women who were taken under the protection of some house of the Order and given an anchorage in a monastery or convent, or adjoining a church

---

32. *Ibid.*, p. 108.
33. *Ibid.*, p. 109.
34. See Epist. 1, 20; analyzed by Leclercq, *op. cit.*, pp. 114ff., *P.L.*, 189, 89-100.

of one of our monasteries. Bd Hazeka (d. 1261), who spent thirty-six years as a recluse in our convent of Sichem, is a case in point.[35]

These recluses observed in their own way the *consuetudines* of the Order. However, it is quite certain that some of the recluses wre indeed profesed members of the Order who had received this permission to live in solitude.[36] Friar B. Griesser, S.O.C., has examined a Rule for Recluses supposedly written by and for Cistercians.[37] The Rule was not in any sense official. It was, he thinks, probably written by a recluse (male) living in an anchorage under Cistercian auspices, and this recluse may perhaps have been himself a professed Cistercian monk. The General Chapter of 1279 (n. 28) forbade giving the habit to recluses who lived under the protection of houses of the Order, but this prohibition was never strictly observed.

That there were departures from Cistercian monasteries to the hermit life goes without saying. At least one English hermit saint, Robert of Knaresborough, first tried his vocation as a lay brother at Newminster, but after a few months decided upon solitude in Knaresborough forest. After his death in 1218 the monks of Fountains were anxious to obtain his relics but did not succeed.

There were Cistercian hermitages in France and Belgium. Dom Leclercq mentions Aiguebelle and Clairmarais as having hermitges in the Middle Ages. He adds that in the reform of the Strict Observance, in the seventeenth and eighteenth centuries, Chambons and Orval possessed hermitages and there was a hermit living an austere life in the shadow of La Trappe in the time of De Rancé.[38]

R. M. Clay in her book *The Hermits and Anchorites of*

---

35. See *Acta Sanctorum*, June, 3, p. 374.
36. Otmar Doerr, *Das Institut der Inclusen in Suddeutschland* (Münster, 1934), pp. 33, 34.
37. *Analecta S.O.C.* (1949), pp. 81ff.
38. See *Studia Monastica* IV, 95.

England (London, 1914) has listed many hermitages and anchorages depending on Cistercian monasteries in England and Wales. It would be useful to consider them here. First of all we find that Revesby, where St Aelred was founder and first abbot, had three hermitages, one of which, according to Clay, dated back to the time of Aelred's abbotship (before 1147). Aelred himself, as abbot of Rievaulx, had to live in a cottage apart, but this was for reasons of health. It must be noted that the fact that a monastery has a hermitage or anchorage does not necessarily mean that one of the monks was a hermit, though certainly this must have been the case more often that we can clearly prove, especially in the early days. But it is quite possible that the "hermit" or "ancre" was simply one who had been taken under the protection of the house. Clay indicates that at least one Revesby hermitage was occupied by a monk. We also hear of a monk of Newminster occupying a hermitage there in the thirteenth century, and the three hermitages belonging to Garendon were occupied, at least sometimes, by monks from the community. Did they then sever their connection with the community as suggested above by Stephen of Lexington?

There is a curious case of an anchorage in a London churchyard (St Giles, Cripplegate) which was given to the Cistercians of Garendon by Edward III. A monk of Saint Albans who transferred to Garendon was for a time a recluse in this London anchorage, but after a year there returned to Saint Albans.[39] We hear of another Cistercian of Garendon applying to live in a hermitage belonging to the Benedictines of Tewkesbury Abbey.[40] This reminds us of the fact that a monk did not necessarily need to confine his desire for solitude to a hermitage belonging to an abbey of his own Order.

---

39. See Clay, *op. cit.*, p. 67.
40. See Clay, *op. cit.*, p. 27.

Other Cistercian monasteries which had one hermitage each were Flaxley, Margam, Grace Dieu, Brueme, Kirkstead, Meaux, and Furness. The case of the Whalley anchorage in Lancashire later became rather notorious, but the ancre there was not a Cisterican. Whalley also had a hermitage, in addition to this reclusory which was in the village churchyard. The Whalley scandal took place in the fifteenth century, which was a late and decadent period in any case. The (female) recluses, particularly one by the name of Isold of Hetton, were not living up to the ideal of the solitary life. However, the records of the case provide us with an interesting insight into the practical working of an anchorage. The foundation was given over to the monks in 1361 by Henry Duke of Lancaster. It consisted of two cottages and the revenue from six hundred and seventy acres of land. In effect, the Abbot of Whalley was simply charged with administering this foundation. He provided a secular priest to take care of the spiritual needs of the two ancresses, and sent weekly provisions of food for the ancresses and their two maids (*i.e.* extern helpers). This included thirty-four loaves of bread and eight gallons of beer. The monks did not even have the right to appoint the ancresses, who were appointed by the duke. The monks paid the duke rent for the anchorage but kept the surplus from the income after the ancresses had been provided for as agreed.

The arrangement at Whalley is probably quite typical of many anchorages and hermitages that one may find, in England and on the Continent, listed as dependencies of Cistercian abbeys. In this case the recluses had nothing whatever to do with the Order. In others, they may have worn the habit of the Order, followed certain customs of the Order, and been directed by monks. However, we do have records, especially in Germany, of nuns of the Order who became recluses. The necrologies of Cistercian monasteries and convents in south Germany indicate that some members of the communities died as recluses. It is curious especially to notice that in the necrologies of monasteries of men we find the record of women recluses who in some cases were certainly nuns of the order. To mention a few of these, found in Doerr:[41] Wettingen, Engelszell, Wilhering, Lilienfeld, and especially Seligenthal, where thirteen recluses are on record, two or three of whom were men, one other being designated as *monialis* and still another as *sor* (sister). In the necrology of Tennenbach (a monastery of men) we find this entry: "*Beata Adelheidis virgo de Tonningen S. Ord. Cist. quae ob amorem Christi prope Thennenbach in fratrum domuncula ad Aspen dicta, ubi adhuc visuntur rudera, inclusa multos annos ibidem sanctam et austeram ducens vitam, sancto fine quievit, sepelitur in Thennenbach.*"[42]

Returning to Britain, Ford Abbey is not listed by Clay as having a hermitage or anchorage, but on the other hand there exists an official document concerning the transit of a monk of Ford to an anchorage at Crewkerne (Somerset) in the fifteenth century. The relations of Ford with the anchorage of Crewkerne were entirely spiritual, and had apparently persisted since the early days of the monastery when a recluse of Crewkerne, Bd Wulfric of Haselbury (d. 1154), was a close friend of at least one of the brothers of the monastery. John of Ford wrote a life of this recluse. Thus the monks of Ford must always have had a respect for the solitary ideal, and the writings of John of Ford are there to show that this was a house where the contemplative life was especially prized and doubtless lived. It is not surprising then that a monk of the Abbey, Dom Robert Cherde, asked and received permission to live as a recluse. The document that has come down to us is a letter to the pastors of neighbouring Somerset villages (including West Coker, evidently next door to T. S. Eliot's East Coker) concerning the steps

41. *Op. cit.*, pp. 97, 98, 100, 103, etc.
42. Doerr, *op. cit.*, p. 97.

to be taken. It confirms our supposition that those who left Cistercian monasteries to become hermits also by that very fact departed from the Order and from the "monastic state."

Six miles from Ford was another Cistercian Abbey, Newenham, which gained possession in 1300 of the anchorage in Axminster churchyard. We do not know if any monk of the Abbey lived there, but there is no reason against supposing that one or other of them might have tried his vocation there. A woman recluse in another village, Colyford, was actually walled in by the Abbot of Newenham, by delegation from the bishop of Exeter. She was one of the few English ancresses actually "blocked up." There is no indication that she was a Cistercian.[43]

One of the Cistercian abbeys on the Scottish border had four hermitage chapels, distinct from its five granges. This was Holm Cultram, in Cumberland. The hermitage of St Cuthbert had two garths containing one acre of land and was occupied by a hermit at the time of the dissolution (1574). Another, St Christian, had one garth of a half acre and was also still occupied in the sixteenth century.[44] However, the most famous attempt at the hermit life in those parts, at least among Cistercians, was the rather unique case of Abbot Adam of Holm Cultram who had been deposed (in the early thirteenth century) in a special visitation by the abbots of Rievaulx and Melrose, for squandering monastery funds in an attempt to get himself elected bishop of Carlisle. He retired to one of the hermitages on his monastery property, but evidently had no solid vocation and in fact went mad. He was brought back to the monastery and imprisoned. He is not to be numbered among the authentic Cistercian recluses!

---

43. See Clay, *op. cit.* p. 141.
44. See G. S. Gilbranks, *Some Records of a Cistercian Abbey, Holm Cultram* (London, n.d.), p. 36.

This very brief and by no means inclusive survey gives some idea of the rich variety of material on the subject that remains to be studied in greater detail. Whatever may have been the objections of a St Bernard to the solitary life, we find not only that the Cistercians of the twelfth to fifteenth and sixteenth centuries were sometimes enthusiastic patrons of recluses and owners and administrators of anchorages and hermitages, but also that monks of the Order retired to hermitages or became recluses, not only in hermitages belonging to houses of the Order but in others belonging to the Benedictines. Thus, in addition to those who relinquished the "monastic state" entirely to become hermits, there is evidence that eremitism existed and flourished within the Cistercian Order as well as among the Benedictines in the Middle Ages.

IV

CONCLUSIONS:

In recent years an unpublished essay by Dom André Louf has once again taken up the question of eremitism in the monastic state. Viewing all the monastic families as members of a single *ordo monasticus*, Dom André came to a tentative conclusion: it should be considered normal for monks with aspirations to solitude to try out their vocation by passing over to one of the eremitical congregations within the *ordo monasticus*, and canonical steps should be taken to make this easy. This tentative suggestion of Dom André Louf would simply accept the monastic Orders and Congregations as they actually are, with their familiar traditions and their current interpretations of the monastic ideal. Supposing that the Cistercian ideal is so purely cenobitic that the hermit life within the Cistercian Order would be unthinkable, then the solution for a Cistercian would be to pass over to the Camaldolese. The aim of Dom André was to win at least a favourable consideration for Cistercians who thought they ought to be solitaries, and he felt that this might be a practical and acceptable way of doing so. It so happens that at the time when the article was written even this moderate view was not found acceptable.

Considered in itself, the view of Dom André has the advantage of fitting into the situation that existed before the Second Vatican Council without appearing to be too bold or unusual. And of course it is true that at any time the passage to a well-established eremitical institute would be an easy and practical solution for monks who would not feel themselves able to embrace a life of total solitude, without special rule and without the support of an organized community of other hermits. On the other hand, it must be frankly admitted that both the Carthusians and the Camaldolese have certain limitations and problems of their own, and it is well enough known that their own members often seek a more satisfactory form of solitary life elsewhere. Carthusians may, for instance, go over to the Camaldolese in order to become recluses there.

Dom Jacques Winandy, in the article already cited, considered two solutions for the problem of the cenobite with a call to solitude: first, exclaustration *ad nutum Sanctae Sedis*, which would allow the monk to withdraw from obedience to his superiors while remaining under obedience directly to the Holy See, and so trying out his vocation as a hermit (under a benevolent bishop). The second solution considered by Dom Winandy was the traditional one of the monk receiving permission to live as a hermit under obedience to his own superiors on the property of his own monastery, and therefore without any rupture of the bonds uniting him to his monastic family. While recognizing the obvious simplicity and the traditional character of this solution, Dom Winandy brought up certain well-founded objections to it. The incomprehension of the monastic community, the possible ill will of a new superior revoking the decision of his predecessor, and other such factors, might make the experiment risky, uncertain and even altogether abortive. There is no question that if the community and abbot are cool toward a hermit experiment, the situation can easily be "rigged" so that its failure will be a foregone conclusion and the familiar thesis *contra eremitas* will once again be manifestly "proved."

It is clear that as long as there exists a general state of suspicion and prejudice toward eremitism in monastic communities, the safest and most practical procedure will be for the monk to leave his community and go elsewhere. He may then either:

(a) transfer to another monastery (for instance a primitive Bendictine community) where the superior is favourable to such experiments. Yet this might entail much the same risk over again. In any case this would hardly be possible unless the monk were well known to the superior in question. In any event a period of trial in the monastery *ad quem* would be necessary. In the case of a change of Order, the present legislation would still demand an indult and a new novitiate. Doubtless steps could be taken to simplify this, and in the revised Code of Canon Law such steps could be considered.

(b) obtain an exclaustration *ad nutum Sanctae Sedis*. But Dom Winandy foresaw that the Congregation might prove unwilling to grant many such exclaustrations and very definite refusals are in fact on record in recent years. . . .

But we still face the question whether or not it is both desirable and possible to revive the hermit life within the monastic state, and under the protection of well-established cenobitic monasteries.

Although in Dom Winandy's article and in the special number of *La Vie Spirituelle* of October 1952, it was taken completely for granted that abbots and abbots general would remain uniformly hostile to all experiments in the solitary life, especially within the Cistercian Order, we are now witnessing a change that can only be accounted for as providential. What the explanation of it may be, one cannot say. It is quite possible that because many American communities have lost as many as three or four members each to Dom Winandy, the Camaldolese, or the Carthusians, this has finally brought home the serious need of reconsidering the hermit question within our own Order. Cistercians cannot help but be impressed by the fact that new primitive Benedictine foundations now assume, as a matter of course, that monks who have a real solitary vocation will be permitted, in due time, to live as hermits in the shadow of the monastery. This is taken for granted as a normal, if rare, development of the monastic vocation.

In any case, not only is the hermit question now open for serious and objective discussion even in the Cistercian Order, but practical proposals are already being made "for a life of complete solitude to be lived on the property of our (Cistercian) monasteries." This would make it possible for well-tested vocations to solitude to find their fulfillment without leaving the religious state, the Order, or the monastery of the monk's profession. It is understood that such vocations would always be quite rare, and the solution to the hermit problem would have to be worked out in a prudent manner, so authentic cenobites would not be disturbed in their own monastic life. It should always remain clear to such cenobites that the hermit life is an unusual way and is not required for monastic perfection. The chief "danger" of a hermit life near the monastery might possibly be the implication that each and every cenobite is thereby challenged to go beyond the common life, by the very presence of a hermit on the property. This is of course not the case. The hermit vocation is always exceptional. However, to be realistic about it, if the hermit really remains a member of the monastic family, which would imply that he might have some continued contact with his community, the others will be able to see that he is no angel and will be able to preserve an objective view of the question, thus avoiding "temptation."

The proposals now being made for the recognition of eremitical solitude as compatible with the Cistercian life are not to be confused with other proposals which are not strictly speaking "eremitical," but which do open up the way to a relative solitude, considered as a necessary element in the common life of the monastery. This relative solitude would consist, for example, in opportunities for a day or so of silence and solitude, apart from the community, in a cabin or chapel somewhere on the monastic property. These days of retreat would be available first of all to officers of the monastery, but doubtless also to other monks who might be considered able to make good use of them.

We are not concerned here with the concrete plans that are now under consideration to restore eremitism within the monastic state. The important thing is the new attitude that must necessarily accompany any such renewal in the life of the *ordo monasticus*. There will certainly not be many hermits living in the shadow of our monasteries. Nevertheless a certain respect for solitude and a mature evaluation of the special needs of certain individuals can be a sign of strength and ripeness in a monastic community. Our monks should learn to treat solitude realistically, not as a delusion of the devil nor yet as a miraculous panacea for all one's troubles, but as a special development which grace demands occasionally in the lives of certain ones. When such a demand really proceeds from grace, then not only the one concerned but also his abbot and his community have certain obligations to see that the demand is met. When the monk-hermit has to work out his vocation on the property of his own monastery, it becomes clear that his struggle and his venture are in some way the concern of all the community. He is called to develop in a way that is somehow relevant to them all, because it is the prolongation not only of his cenobitic life but of theirs. This development will always be difficult, even hazardous. The monk who embarks on it does so at considerable risk, and the fact of his doing so should not constitute a boast that he is somehow superior to the rest of the community. On the contrary, he will be brought face to face with his own weakness and his own poverty in ways that would perhaps be quite unbearable without special grace and the help of the community's prayers and understanding.

The problem and paradox of these hermit vocations, which will always tend to make them seem disturbing and sometimes even scandalous, is that though they are a normal fruit of the monastic life they are also unusual, even in the sense of implying a break in continuity in the life of the one who is called to be a hermit. Obviously, the normal monastic life does not simply and continuously grow into a hermit's solitude. He who is called to this solitude is called, perhaps abruptly, to start on a new path. He receives a new vocation, which is certainly a perfection of his former calling, but is nonetheless a new breakthrough of grace, demanding that he now abandon a certain security and familiar pattern that he has created for himself out of years of faithful monastic observance. In a very real sense he has to begin all over again at the beginning and this time without the help of a novice-master, a wise guide, and encouraging companions. If he feels himself to be regarded as a kind of apostate, or as an eccentric or as a deluded fool, it will not make things any easier for him. But this lack of understanding may itself be an element willed by God to confirm his solitary vocation.[45] Needless to say, the argument that the hermit is sitting around "doing nothing" and that his soli-

---

45. Cf. Dom P. Doyère in *La Vie Spirituelle*, October 1952, pp. 253-4.

tary existence has ceased to have any meaning or justification is in itself no more valid than the same superficial arguments proposed against the cenobitic life by people in the world.

The purpose of these pages has been to show that there has been a constant tradition, in Western monasticism, and even within the Cistercian Order, which has not only recognized the rights of the solitary vocation in theory, but has even permitted certain simple, concrete solutions within the juridical and institutional framework of the monastic state. It has never been unusual, it has never been an aberration, for monks to seek and find solitude in the shadow of their own monastery, without having recourse to indults, and without giving up their monastic vows. This remains in itself the simplest, the most practical, and the most traditional monastic solution. But of course it cannot be worked out in practice without a great deal of prudence, tact, charity, and understanding.

Let us hope that, with a more frank and objective view of the situation, it may now become easier both for subjects and superiors to discuss this matter in a spirit of openness and sincerity, completely disposed to bow to God's will in whatever way it may manifest itself. We can only regret that this problem has too often been fought out, in the past, between minds completely closed on both sides, in a *dialogue de sourds* that has naturally been without issue.

If the question is now, we hope, to be discussed more openly and with less passion, monks will have to recognize clearly that no one can ever claim as a *strict right* that his demand to live as a hermit on the monastery property *must* be heard by superiors, in spite of all their objections. One of the most telling indications of a false "vocation" to solitude will perhaps be the unreasonableness, the arrogance and the impatience with which the candidate might presume to assert his claims without brooking any contradiction. Obviously, in order to meet this eventuality, those concerned with establishing norms by which to judge solitary vocations, will want to make these norms fairly strict in order that unreasonable demands may be eliminated right away. Of course there remains a possibility of erroneous judgement, but the candidate in that case could always have recourse to a *transitus.* Thus it remains altogether likely that even admitting the possiblity of a monk becoming a hermit on the property of his monastery, there will still be some who, for one reason or another, will have to seek their solution by transferring to the Carthusians, the Camaldolese, or other communities, or else even by leaving the monastic state. But much will have been gained if at least one or two genuine solitary vocations are seen to develop and grow out of our common monastic life and flourish with the protection and love of the monastic community. We must conclude by remembering that this will always be God's work and not man's.

Having begun with a quotation from a writer who signed himself "Théophile Reclus" and who sounds remarkably like Dom Winandy, let us end with another quotation from the same writer in the same article:

> The hermit is a sign of God, destined to remind men of the transitoriness of this world and to present to their gaze an image of the world to come. More than in any other vocation, perhaps, is the initiative in this one entirely from God. . . . And does not God have the right to act thus? Who then will be presumptuous enough to demand an account from him? It is more fitting to adore in awe the mystery of his designs.[46]

---

46. *La Vie Spirituelle*, October 1952, p. 241.

IS THE CONTEMPLATIVE LIFE
FINISHED?

Is the Contemplative Life finished?

"Contemplative" is a bad word. When we talk about ourselves, monks, as contemplatives, we come face to face with the problem that we are not more than contemplatives. We are not prophets. We are failing in the prophetic aspect of our vocation. Why? Perhaps because we belong to a Christianity so deeply implicated in a society which has outlived its spiritual vitality and yet is groping for a new expression of life in crisis. Our monasteries are not fulfilling any kind of prophetic vocation in the modern world. Whether we should be able to do that or not is another matter. The prophetic charism is a gift of God, not a duty of man.

But on the other hand, if the gift has not been given, perhaps we who had the call have not prepared ourselves. It seems to me that contemplatives should be able to say to modern man something about God that answers the profoundly important and significant accusation of Marx against religion. Marx said religion inevitably leads to the alienation of man. It is not fulfillment but opium. Man in his worship of God divests himself of his own powers and of his own dignity and attributes these to an invisible and remote God and then begs God to grant them, give them back to him bit by bit, in retail packages. But that is not the case. We are learning more and more that the denial of God is really the denial of man. Yet, on the other hand, the affirmation of God is the true affirmation of man. Barth somewhere said: "Merely to talk about man in a loud voice is not to talk about God." Unless we really affirm God, we do not affirm man. Unless we affirm God as the One who calls man into existence and to freedom and to love which is the fulfillment of that freedom—unless we affirm this God, we fail to affirm that without which man's life has no meaning.

Monks ought to be able to reassure the modern world that in the struggle between thought and existence we are on the side of existence, not on the side of abstraction. But can we honestly affirm this? I don't know.

A great deal of monastic life and "contemplative spirituality" is not necessarily abstract in a philosophical sense, but it is an artificial behaviour in which thought, embodied in ritual forms, opposes itself to the concrete facts of existence. Do we make a fetish out of subjecting the realities of human existence to ritual forms and legalisms, to convince ourselves that in so doing we are leading spiritual and contemplative lives?

We monks should be able to reassure modern man that God is the source and the guarantee of our freedom and not simply a force standing over us to limit our freedom.

In the conflict between law and freedom, God is on the side of freedom. That is a scandalous statement! But it is the New Testament! How are we going to affirm to the modern world the scandal of the New Testament? It is here that we confront the seriousness of our *prophetic* as distinct from our *contemplative* calling.

Surely this is the "message" the monk should give the world. But to what extent can monks express this? We are, so it would seem, as committed to law as anybody. More than others! We multiply laws. We live a highly mediated existence in which at any moment rule and rite can substitute for authentic experience and encounter.

Our encounter with God should be, at the same time, the discovery of our own deepest freedom. If we never encounter God, our freedom never fully develops. It develops only in the existential encounter between the Christian and God, or between man and God—because not only Christians encounter God. Every man at some point in his life encounters God, and many who are not Christians have responded to God better than Christians. Our encounter with God, our response to his Word, is the drawing forth and calling out of our deepest freedom, our true identity.

Prayer

To understand prayer properly, we have to see in it this encounter of our freedom emerging from the depths of nothingness and undevelopment, at the call of God. Prayer is freedom and affirmation growing out of nothingness into love. Prayer is the flowering of our inmost freedom, in response to the Word of God. Prayer is not only dialogue with God: it is the communion of our freedom with his ultimate freedom, his infinite spirit. It is the elevation of our limited freedom into the infinite freedom of the divine spirit, and of the divine love. Prayer is the encounter of our freedom with the all-embracing charity that knows no limit and knows no obstacle. Prayer is an emergence into this area of infinite freedom. Prayer then is not an abject procedure although sometimes it may spring from our abjection.

Of course, we have to face the existential reality of our wretchedness, nothingness, and abjection because it is there that our prayer begins. It is out of this nothingness that we are called into freedom. It is out of this darkness that we are called into light. Therefore, we need to recognize this as our true starting point. Otherwise our prayer is not authentic. But we are called *out* of this nothingness, darkness, and alienation and frustration, into communion and intimacy with God, in his freedom. That is the meaning of prayer. Prayer therefore is not just simply a matter of thrusting ourselves down into a position of abjection, and grovelling in servile submission asking God for things that are already our own. That is the picture that Marx in his idea of religious alienation gives us. Prayer is not something that is meant to maintain us in servility and helplessness. We take stock of our own wretchedness at the beginning of prayer in order to rise beyond it and above it to infinite freedom and infinite creative love in God.

Prayer infallibly does this if we believe it and if we understand its true dimensions. The great problem of prayer arises from the fact that if we take the alienated view we remain fixed in our own ego and we are no longer able to go out from ourselves into freedom. If we remain in our ego, clenched upon ourselves, trying to draw down to ourselves gifts which we then incorporate in our own limited selfish life, then prayer does remain servile. Servility has its root in self-serving. Servility, in a strange way, really consists in trying to make God serve our own needs. We have to try to say to modern man something about the fact that authentic prayer enables us to emerge from our servility into freedom in God, because it no longer strives to manipulate him by superstitious "deals."

Good Souls

Suppose, for a moment, that the term "contemplative" has a value and can be retained: in what sense are we contemplatives? In what sense are there real contemplatives in our monasteries? Obviously there are, especially among the older generation, a lot of people who have been and are authentic men of prayer. Yet so few, so very few seem really to be deeply *contemplative*. They are more what you would call "good souls." They are worthy products of the religious system that has prevailed up to now, good regular people who have been faithful to their obligations. They have put their obligations before everything else and come to choir on time. They have been rewarded with satisfaction and peace. They have a kind of solid interior life going. Over the years they have acquired a certain experience and a deep love of God—no question about that. What they have apparently failed to develop is real depth of insight and a real fullness of life. Few have a real depth of spiritual consciousness and a real depth of interior experience. If they have, it is something that they are absolutely unable to articulate, something they are not even aware of. And of course, that is as it should be. But are they contemplatives? Or *should* they be?

You expect to find simple and deep people in the contemplative life. The true contemplative should not necessarily have much to say about his contemplative life. The business of articulating it can be a charism or it can be a delusion. But the fact remains that there is something to the articulation of this deep experience. One should be able to teach it to others, to make others understand what it is, and help them to attain it. That is the question that is raised by this message of contemplatives of the modern world. Do we have any depth of experience that we can communicate to the modern world in its own terms? Or should we just asume that the modem world is so far out that it does not deserve any message from us?

Is the contemplative merely there to create a sense of stability, devoutness, piety, and peace? Is his the message of confidence that what has been is still going on and will continue to go on? He may indeed comfort you with such a message, but when he stops talking and when you start reflecting on all he has said, you realize that what has been is *not* going to go on. What has been has ended. We hope certainly that some of the qualities of that kind of interior life will continue. We would hate to lose the qualities of simplicity and devotion and piety and all that. But the message of our venerable and ancient system is not good enough. Its emphasis is almost always on something secondary. The emphasis is not on the deep realities of life. You may say our contemplative speaks of the cross and so forth—well, the cross is certainly not secondary. But it is too often seen from the point of view of the secondary. So much is taken for granted, so much is assumed. When the cross is spoken of in the context of what one might call *milieu* Catholicism (that is to say in which a Catholic *milieu* is taken for granted), then we assume that all the big things are taken care of by the *milieu*, and we are only responsible for minor details. The basic problems of life are taken for granted as having been solved years ago and nobody even raises them any more. In that context the cross, instead of being a deep mystery which shakes the very depths of man's being in death and resurrection, becomes a matter of not blowing your top when somebody is late. The cross is a matter of being patient when you have to wait outside the abbot's office.

The "contemplative life" is then reduced to little things like: learning to become a man of interior prayer by making good use of the moments when you just have to kick your heels waiting for something to happen—or for someone to provide something you need (and will maybe never get)—or for someone in authority to notice you are there and pat you on the head and say you are a good boy. The cross is emptied of all seriousness by this kind of fiddling around, even though from a certain point of view it is not fiddling around. It can only appear serious within the context of a well-established, stable society, a Christian bourgeois society which is firmly built on its foundation which shall never be shaken. But that has ended. The foundations are thoroughly shaken. That kind of society no longer exists. We're living in a world in revolution. The foundations of everything familiar are menaced, and if in the midst of this the mystery of the cross means practising patience and offering it up and so forth when you're sitting in front of a man's office in order to get permission to do something that you ought to have sense enough to do for yourself, it becomes ludicrous in the eyes of the modern world. Therefore if the message of contemplatives to the modem world springs from something as trival as this—even though it may be using big words like cross, death, resurrection, prayer, contemplation, vision—it's going to be ridiculous! It's not going to touch anybody. They don't want any part of it. If this is contemplation, then we might as well pick up our marbles and go home.

The Sacrifice of Security

Let us now face the question of how badly we need renewal and how little the renewal is really taking place. We don't even know where to begin this renewal. It has to be our renewal, not just simply a renewal which introduces the active life into the cloister. We cannot seek the same kind of renewal as is sought in the active orders because we have a different job to do in the Church. True, we're all going back to the gospel; but nowhere in the gospel are we told that the mystery of the cross and the mystery of the Resurrection and so forth are reduced to the little formalities to which we have reduced them. Nor is renewal simply a question of broadening out within the enclosure wall and just fitting a more liberal and more relaxed spirituality into the framework of offices and duties. Nor is it a matter of unending dialogue about those same offices and duties. Renewal means much more than that. You who are interested enough in this matter to be reading and I who am trying to develop these ideas are all involved together in a very crucial search for the realities of renewal. We are trying to see what demands are really going to be made on us. We want to estimate those demands properly and objectively. We want to be ready to pay the price—and the price here is not going to be just a matter of gritting our teeth and following orders that we instinctively realize to be beside the point!

It may be the price of sacrificing our security, *sacrificing the psychological stability we have built on foundations that we do not dare to examine.* We have to examine those foundations even though it will mean unrest, even though it will mean loss of peace, even though it will mean disturbance and anguish, even though it may mean the radical shaking of structures.

Certain structures need to be shaken, certain structures have to fall. We need not be revolutionaries within our institutions. Nowadays one sees too much of the neurotic rebel in the cloister, the neurotic who is interminably complaining about everything and has absolutely no intention of substituting anything positive for all this negation, the person who is always discontented and automatically throwing the blame for everything on somebody else—we don't need that. But on the other hand we don't want to go to the other extreme and just simply be ostriches, refusing to see that these institutions are in many respects outdated. and that perhaps renewal may mean the collapse of some institutional structures and starting over again with a whole new form.

There have perhaps been some unwise attempts at experimental foundations. In a few months they have proved to be pathetic: but that does not mean that we must not continue searching for new ways. On the other hand (now I really am rambling), we have to remember that there is an order in these things and that you do not sit down and start writing a new rule first thing of all. The writing of new rules should be the last thing of all. What one needs to do is to start a conversion and a new life oneself, in so far as one can. Thus, my new life and my contribution to a renewal in monasticism begin within myself and in my own daily life. My work for renewal takes place strictly in my own situation here, not as a struggle with the institution but in an effort to renew my life of prayer in a whole new context, with a whole new understanding of what the contemplative life means and demands. Creativity has to begin with me and I can't sit here wasting time urging the monastic institution to become creative and prophetic. To begin with there is really not much change to be expected within the framework of the institution. It can change so much and no more. After that the structure won't take any more change. So it is useless lamenting over the fact that it can't be more creative. It is useless lamenting over the fact that the best people continue to leave and it is useless building hopes on illusory token changes which are after all a little petty. What each one of us has to do, what I have to do, is to buckle down and really start investigating new possibilities in our own lives; and if the new possibilities mean radical changes, all right. Maybe we need radical changes for which we may have to struggle and sweat some blood. Above all we must be more attentive to God's way and God's time, and give everything when it is really demanded.

We, the supposedly "contemplative" monks, need renewal as much as everybody else and we've got to do it ourselves. We have to find out for ourselves what we're supposed to be doing. We cannot sit around waiting for somebody else to tell us. You who read this are yourselves studying possibilities of renewal. Let me encourage you as a brother to forget about other people who are supposed to help you do it. Do it yourself with the help of the Holy Spirit. Find out what you are really looking for in the spiritual life. What did you really come to the cloister for? Why do you want to be a Carmelite, a Trappist, a contemplative? What are you seeking? Are you seeking security or are you seeking God? Are you seeking pleasant experiences or are you seeking the truth?

Are we seeking the truth that is to make us free? Are we seeking the truth of Christ? Are we responding to the Word of God which breaks through all structures of human life and institutions? These are the things which we have to ask ourselves. We can hardly expect others to answer these things for us!

The important thing for us is to clarify our aims and to

rethink not only the accidentals but even the essentials of the contemplative life—in the sense of re-thinking our aims, our motives, and ends. What do we come to the contemplative life for? Each of us may have a different answer. And let us not make the mistake of imagining ourselves re-thinking the life in order to *re-legislate* it. In other words let us not kid ourselves by talking now and living later. If our re-thinking is valid it is also a re-living. Don't let's get lost in words. Let's live now. Let us not project ourselves too far ahead. Let us live in the present. Our re-thinking of the contemplative life is part of our present contemplation. Our new life will emerge from authenticity now. This is not merely an empty moment of transition. We are not in an interval of dynamic reconstruction in which we are simply going to put back together again a static life in which we will rest. Our rest is in the reconstruction itself. Transition is also fullness. We can have a certain personal fullness even when the changing institution is provisional, and we have to learn to be able to be contemplatives in the midst of the dynamic, in the midst of movement.

We can do this without being obsessed by the movement, without being too conscious of ourselves in movement. We can live happily in change, not worrying about change. Change is one of the big facts of all life. If we're not able to be contemplatives in the midst of change, if we insist on being contemplatives in some completely stable situation which we imagine we are going to construct in the future, then we're never going to be contemplatives.

So let's move on in a quiet, confident way and be content. Let us not try to be too conscious of ourselves moving and not demand that everything be secure. Let us live first in Christ, fully open to his Spirit, unconcerned about institutional security, free from all care for ideal structures that will never be built, and content with the Dark Night of faith in which alone we are truly secure because truly free!

Contemplative Life

What do we think the contemplative life is? How do we conceive it? As a life of withdrawal, tranquillity, retirement, silence? Do we keep ourselves from action and change in order to learn techniques for entering into a kind of static present reality which is there and which we have to learn how to penetrate? Is contemplation an objective static "thing," like a building, for which there is a key? Do you hunt for this key, find it, then unlock the door and enter? Well, that is a valid image from a certain point of view, but it isn't the only image.

The contemplative life isn't something objective that is "there" and to which, after fumbling around, you finally gain access. The contemplative life is a dimension of our subjective existence. Discovering the contemplative life is a new self-discovery. One might say it is the flowering of a deeper identity on an entirely different plane from a mere psychological discovery, a paradoxical new identity that is found only in loss of self. To find one's self by losing one's self: that is part of "contemplation." Remember the Gospel, "He who would save his life must lose it."

The contemplative experience originates from this totally new kind of awareness of the fact that we are most truly ourselves when we lose ourselves. We become ourselves when we lose ourselves in Christ. Our contemplative vocation can become perverse and selfish if we are surreptitiously using tricks and bad faith. Bad faith for us consists in trying to play around with this concept of finding ourselves by losing ourselves. Bad faith wants to learn some trick of losing ourselves so that we find ourselves and we come out on top in the end. This is one source of the self-deception and frustration that are so frequent in the contemplative life. Consequently, one of the basic rules is that it is always a gift of God. It is always something for which we must learn how to wait. But it is also something which we must learn

93

to *expect actively.* The secret of the contemplative life is *ability for active awareness*, an active and expectant awareness where the activity is a deep personal response on a level which is, so to speak, beyond the faculties of the soul.

Contemplative prayer is a deep interior activity in the very roots of our being in response to God who has the intiative and yet draws us into certain very subtle forms of obedient initiative on our own side. This combination of initiative and expectant passivity is different in different people. So many things enter into it. In the renewal of the contemplative life we must not narrow down the possibilities for individual development as we have done in the past.

In the past, the contemplative life was proposed in a rather rigid, formal sort of way. You entered the contemplative life by making a list of things which you were going to drop, so to speak. You took the world and all its possibilities and you just crossed everything off the list. You crossed off the joys of human love, you crossed off the joys of art, music, secular literature, enjoyment of beauties of nature, enjoyment of natural recreation, sports, swimming. All these things, you just discarded: and when you had crossed everyting off the list, then the one great thing was left, the *unum necessarium*, the one thing necessary!

I think we have radically to re-evaluate our whole view of this "one thing necessary." The one thing necessary is not that which is left when everything is crossed off, but it is perhaps that which includes and embraces everything else, that which is arrived at when you've added up everything and gone far beyond. I don't want to put it in a quantitative way, however. Of course you understand, in reality the crossing-off process was supposed to be an elimination of a quantitative view, in order to get down to a strictly qualitative approach. You were supposed to end up, not with what was most but with what was best. I think we should aim for the most as well as the best but not the most and the best outside ourselves. The most and the best in ourselves. Here I think we need a great deal of subtlety and flexibility in recognizing the real vital possibilities of each individual in the contemplative life. Contemplative discipline is both hard and flexible. The contemplative life should be a life in which there is austerity. There has to be a real challenge. It's got to be a tough life. This business of just softening up the contemplative life is foolish. In fact it means the end of all contemplation. But the contemplative life has to be tough in such a way that it is also livable. The toughness of the contemplative life should not be that restricting toughness which arbitrarily rules out good possibilities. It should be a toughness that tones us up to meet new possibilities, the unexpected, that for which we have not been previously capable, for which we have not been previously ready.

In other words, the toughness of the contemplative life was to lift us above ourselves, above our capacities. A life of self-transcendence must be hard—hard and rewarding, not hard and frustrating.

This should give us some insight into the new way of asceticism, a rewarding hardness, a hardness that brings you out. The kind of hardness you get in football when you have to really play. So a re-evaluation of our aims in the contemplative life should, I think, take this new form of not simply assuming to begin with that we have crossed off all kinds of possibilities.

Art comes to mind here. By "art" I don't mean fiddling around, please! There is always a temptation to diddle around in the contemplative life, making itsy-bitsy statues. If this is wanted as a legitimate recreation, as a relaxation, or as occupational therapy, let's be honest and call it occupational therapy.

Yet art in the contemplative life can really open up new capacities and new areas in the person of the contemplative. Everything depends on how it is used. The real key is guidance and direction and selectivity. The contemplative life is extremely selective. One of the things that has ruined the contemplative life has been the levelling process, which has eliminated this selective quality, this capacity for creative personal judgement in special cases. The contemplative life has become a kind of assembly line on which everybody is put together according to one pattern. This is utterly deadly, and of course it kills selective judgement.

The lack of qualitative judgement, of taste, of personal discrimination, of openness to new possibilities, is bound up with one great defect—a failure of imagination. Our prayer itself is poor in imagination. The pragmatic and legalistic approach to the religious life in general, and to the contemplative life in particular, has resulted in a dreadful banality. Creativity has not been desired, imagination has been discouraged, and emphasis has been on submission of will, accepting the incomprehensible stupidity of a mechanical existence instead of thinking of a realistic way of improving things. But the solution is not in changing observances and practices, or in changing laws. The solution lies deeper, in the life of prayer. If what goes on inside our minds and hearts is banal, trivial, petty, and unimaginative, we cannot be creative in our outer works. So much that is new and experimental is proving to be a frightful let-down because it is so second-rate, so superficial, so imitative. And so much of it is in the worst possible taste—as many of our old pieties were also in the worst taste.

The Imagination

Let us consider now whether the imagination has a place in the contemplative life. The imagination is one of the things we have tended to rule out of the contemplative life, largely in reaction against its formalized use in systematic meditation. Most of us, I suppose, ran into a period of revolt against the formalized use of the imagination in systematic "composition of place" and that sort of thing.

Here we must distinguish. I would say that a deliberate use of imagination in prayer might perhaps be a good thing for people who have weak imaginations, whose imagination has never been developed in any way at all. They might profitably be encouraged to exercise their imagination a little. But they must exercise it, not just follow a book written by someone whose imagination has gone dead.

I mentioned a moment ago ruling out everything in order to arrive at contemplation. Those of us who have read St John of the Cross remember the chapters of the Ascent of Mount Carmel where he strongly emphasizes the fact that anything that can be imagined or apprehended by the inner or outer senses has nothing to do with God. Whatever can be "seen" cannot be God. Therefore it is better to withdraw from imaginative activity in contemplative prayer, and of course that's true.

On the other hand, imagination has an important part to play in our lives. We all know that when imagination is not constructively used, is not creatively used, it uses itself destructively. It works whether we want it to or not, and one of the places where we all run into imagination is in distractions. Because of the constant struggle with distractions we tend to take an excessively negative view of the imagination.

Some people cannot abide to have distractions. Their imagination works automatically, creating distractions, and then they hate themselves for it. Their whole life is reduced to a despairing struggle with distractions which, of course, makes distractions worse.

Distractions are produced by the imagination, and in many people distractions are worse because their imagination has nothing constructive, nothing creative to work on. For some people the great cross of distraction and imagination is the fact that imagination, when not constructively used, has a tendency to fix itself on what we call "impure" images. Now, perhaps I might mention in passing that this should just be ignored. To begin with, no image is impure. It is neither pure nor impure. There is nothing "wrong" or "dirty" about images. The wrong lies in a disordered affection of the will. A mere image is never impure, it's neutral. The thought of a part of a body is not impure, it just *is*, that's all.

I am speaking about imagination that doesn't have any constructive outlet. It is important for us to find creative outlets and work for the imagination. Imagination has to be sublimated, not necessarily in prayer but certainly elsewhere. Where are some of the fields where we can find work for the imagination? Well, obviously the first thing that suggests itself is in reading the Bible. There is plenty in the Bible that appeals to the imagination, and the psalms are full of imagination. Anything poetic, anything literary, anything creative, in that sense, is full of imagination.

Imagination has the creative task of making symbols, joining things together in such a way that they throw new light on each other and on everything around them. The imagination is a discovering faculty, a faculty for seeing relationships, for seeing meanings that are special and even quite new. The imagination is something which enables us to discover unique present meaning in a given moment of our life. Without imagination the contemplative life can be extremely dull and fruitless.

Remember also that imagination doesn't just create fictions. These are real meanings that the imagination discovers, not just delusions. Yet of course they can be delusory and this is another problem. You see, with imagination you also need judgement. Imagination needs to be corrected with a certain intellectual estimate first of all on a prudential level, and then also even on an artistic level.

We have to consider the artistic truth of things that are

brought together by imagination. This, in fact, is what is wrong very often with a crazy imagination. There can be a beauty in a deliberate grotesque and bizarre effect, but then one must be able to be conscious of this. But when imagination goes haywire in the contemplative life people get slightly nutty. They come to you with grotesque illusions, idiotic and often extremely complicated hang-ups—visions, voices, pseudo-prophecies, and take them very seriously in the wrong way. This is work of the imagination, and from a certain point of view you can regard it as creative in a nutty sort of way. But they are drawing wrong conclusions from it. They are rationalizing and verbalizing.

The contemplative life should not lead us just to suppress the imagination in order to get more pure messages from God. We must allow both for a contemplative prayer in which the imagination has little or no part, and for a creative, imaginative, genuinely poetic side in our life. Our imagination must be able to click and find correspondences, symbols, and meanings. It should point up new meanings. It should create nuclei of meaning around which everything can collect significantly.

So when we talk about using the imagination in this particular way we imply a certain training or discipline of the imagination. This training should not be a matter of exterior compulsion, the domination of imagination by intellect and will. There are times of course when that is necessary. But the imagination should be allowed a certain freedom to browse around, find its own spontaneous material and work with that material. The intelligence and will should go along with it meanwhile—permissively, so to speak.

The training of the imagination implies a certain freedom and this freedom implies a certain capacity to choose and to find its own appropriate nourishment. Thus in the interior life there should be moments of relaxation, freedom, and "browsing." Perhaps the best way to do this is in the midst of nature, but also in literature. Perhaps also a certain amount of art is necessary, and music. Of course we have to remember our time is limited and first things have to come first. We can't spend too much time just listening to music.

You also need a good garden, and you need access to the woods, or to the sea. Get out in those hills and really be in the midst of nature a little bit! That is not only legitimate, it is in a certain way necessary. Don't take your cloister concept too materially. Of course now I may be running into all kinds of problems with constitutions. But the woods and nature should be part of your solitude, and if it's not periodically part of your solitude I think the law should be changed.

Liberating the Imagination

The contemplative life should liberate and purify the imagination, which passively absorbs all kinds of things without our realizing it; liberate and purify it from the influence of so much violence done by the bombardment of social images. There is a kind of contagion that affects the imagination unconsciously much more than we realize. It emanates from things like advertisements and from all the spurious fantasies that are thrown at us by our commercial society. These fantasies are deliberately intended to exercise a powerful effect on our conscious and subconscious minds. They are directed right at our instincts and appetites, and there is no question but that they exercise a real transforming power on our whole psychic structure. The contemplative life should liberate us from that kind of pressure, which is really a form of tyranny. It should subject our imagination passively to *natural* influences. There has been in the past a certain danger of unnatural influences and sick fantasies in the cloister itself. So often in cloistered life we have seen people simply imprisoned in an atmosphere of total ugliness, the pious ugliness of sick statuary and sentimental holy cards.

There has been a great deal of house cleaning in various religious Orders, and in the Church in general, in regard to bad art and bad influences on the imagination. In training the imagination we should work with the inexhaustible supply of images in the Bible, for example. Take a certain passage of the Bible and simply be fully conscious, completely aware of what is addressed to the imagination. *See* it and *grasp* it and *experience* it with the inner senses. Liturgy, too, is a favoured means (at least ideally) for this education of all the senses and of the whole man.

Our imagination should be spontaneous but it should not always be completely unconscious or instinctive. Certainly a contemplative has to be liberated from a completely mechanical imagination. The imagination needs a certain critical reflection, a certain conscious awareness, a certain, let us say, conscious freedom of judgement in its exercise. The healthy imagination is one which can spontaneously move itself to what it likes *better*—consciously awarely, not *self-*consciously. The imagination moves in a state of conscious awareness but not in self-conscious examination of itself; not watching itself act but simply acting in full and joyous consciousness of the fact that it acts.

When reading the Bible your imagination should be distinctly aware of the images, the pictures presented to it. Besides taking account of these separate elements, it should also see how they are fused together in a symbolic unity, in what the Germans call a *Gestalt*, a form made by things converging in a new living unity. Train yourself to see those things when you are reading the Bible.

Don't think that every time you read the Bible you must always be getting the loftiest possible theological sense! In the Bible, theology is embedded in material images and if you don't see the images you don't get the theological sense completely. The theological sense is not only an intellectual message addressed purely to the mind, a purely speculative meaning. There are meanings in the Bible which are communicated in concrete, living, material imagery, in material elements, fire, water, and so on. One has to be sensible, sensitive, sensitized to the material qualities of these things in order to get the divine message.

Catholic Pessimism

The English Benedictine Dom Sebastian Moore, in a book called *God Is a New Language*, frankly discusses what he calls "a Catholic neurosis." He hits some nails pretty squarely on the head. He is talking (among other things) about life in Catholic institutions. He talks about how a layman teaching in a Catholic school may complain quite justly of the fact that he is dealt with in a very dishonest and devious sort of way by the religious who are running the school. They won't meet things squarely. Instead of telling him directly and frankly about something, they try to get it to him through a lot of other people. Then, they think, there won't be any argument!

That happens in monasteries, too. Superiors, not wanting to run into open conflict with subjects, don't tell them directly what they want to tell them. They avoid confrontation and try to get it to the subject indirectly or by hints. You get rumours about what the superior thinks rather than hearing from him personally. And you are somehow expected to act on the rumour. An "obedience" based on this kind of thing is pretty equivocal! But that is not the point. The point that he brings up is of great value for contemplatives because it is one of the curses of our cloistered life.

Sebastian Moore talks about a kind of Catholic pessimism. It is related to the disgust and despair and discouragement we get in the contemplative life. This sense of frustration and hopelessness is due to the conditions of the life. This is something that we've really got to learn how to deal with. He says: "The effect of being continually exposed to the truth which is doing one no good is distressing to the soul. There can even result a kind of unbelief, an exhaustion of the spirit which is all the worse for being partly unconscious."

He relates this to the medieval concept of *acedia*, a kind of spiritual lassitude approaching despair. This is one of the curses of the contemplative life and we have not even begun to know how to deal with it. "The effect of being continually exposed to the truth which is doing one no good!"

Now let's make a distinction here. Does he mean continually exposed to an *ideal* which is held up before us and which, we feel, is doing us no good? An occupational disease of contemplatives consists in this unconscious conviction that we are in the presence of wonderful spiritual values which aren't reaching us. Somehow we are failing them, we are never quite measuring up.

One of the ways of reacting is to deny that this is happening at all or to get around it in some equivocal way—by verbalizing or rationalizing. The classic example of this is the old Latin choir and the classic "solution" is to make an act of pure intention. The will to mean it is equivalent to meaning it even though you do not understand. Thus it becomes a sacrifice of praise, the prayer of the Church, etc. There is of course some truth in this but not enough truth to serve as a solid foundation for one's *whole contemplative life*! Now, the key word here is *alienation*. To be alienated is to be a prisoner of something in which you cannot possibly take an active personal part. This accounts for the kind of choir neurosis that people get into. There is a deep resistance that gradually develops against a thing in which one is participating and yet *not* participating.

This is aggravated by an over-emphasis on the ideal and on the wonderful values that are present—that we are missing. The ideal is extolled and magnified until it gets to be so great, so superhuman, that we *can't* participate in it. Besides, it is all presented in a completely abstract sort of way. We see with our mind that these values are there. We're told that these values are there and we believe it. We're constantly reproached for not measuring up, and we believe that too. We become obsessed by it. This is all done in an abstract sort of way so that you have to have a peculiar kind of intellect and a peculiar kind of will to be able to measure up to this inhuman challenge. You have to be able to believe in pure, disembodied, mathematical will-power (helped by an abstract kind of grace!). Hence the sense of awful futility, of being confronted with something that we're not measuring up to. Here is this immense truth and it is not getting through to us!

And yet, on the other hand, there is a great deal of this truth around that *could* get through to us. But we are not paying attention because we have not been trained to pay attention. We would even feel guilty for paying attention to it. We think it is not supernatural enough! Here again we neglect the imaginative content of some of the things that we live with all the time, the Bible for example. The imaginative and human appeal of the Bible and the liturgy is something that we completely bypass. We do not pay attention to it because we suppose that it is something inferior and we "want only the best." So we bypass a value which we *could* participate in and could experience. Take the joy of singing in choir. Of course that gets knocked out of us because when we sing we are apt to ruin the whole choir! Still, that is what the choir is for. People should be able to enjoy the singing and enjoy what's going on! But perhaps when they enjoy it, they make it intolerable for other people, so there is a problem. We have to face the fact; but we would be able to get to a lot of these values quite easily and quite simply if we would just be natural about them.

But we are told *not* to be natural. If you are taking a *natural* pleasure in something, it is not *supernatural* and that's wrong. I think we should be able to take these natural pleasures and realize that they're not opposed to the super- natural at all. They are a means of entering into contact with the real spiritual values which are given to us. We should not be afraid to make use of them. Then we might better face this situation of frustrating alienation in the reli- gious life, this feeling that we're constantly exposed to an immense truth which is not coming through and is not getting to us. We're not responding to it on levels on which we could respond. We are attempting to respond on impos- sible levels. This is a highly destructive situation, and when a person lives under this day after day the whole thing gets to be incomparably sick. People saying over and over again what these great values are, etc., and nobody experiencing them at all. For you realize that the person who is giving you this enthusiastic pep talk doesn't experience them either. Better just to smell a flower in the garden or some- thing like that than to have an unauthentic experience of a much higher value. Better to honestly enjoy the sunshine or some light reading than to claim to be in contact with something that one is not in contact with at all.

So, therefore, I would say that it is very important in the contemplative life *not to overemphasize the contemplation.* If we constantly overemphasize those things to which access is inevitably quite rare, we overlook the ordinary authentic real experiences of everyday life as real things to enjoy, things to be happy about, things to praise God for. But the ordinary realities of everyday life, the faith and love with which we live our normal human lives, provide the founda- tion on which we build those higher things. If there is no foundation, then we have nothing at all! How can we relish the higher things of God if we cannot enjoy some simple little thing that comes along as a gift from God! We should enjoy these things and then we will be able to go on to more rare experiences. Take the enjoyment of our daily bread.

Bread is true, isn't it? Well, I don't know. Maybe one of the troubles with modern life is that bread is no longer true bread. But around here, in this monastery, we have pretty good bread. Things that are good are good, and if one is responding to that goodness one is in contact with a truth from which one is getting something. The truth is doing us good. The truth of the sunshine, the truth of the rain, the truth of the fresh air, the truth of the wind in the trees, these are *truths*. And they are always accessible! Let us be exposed to these in such a way that they do us good because these are very accessible forms of truth, and if we allow ourselves to be benefited by the forms of truth that are really accessible to us instead of rejecting and disparaging and despising them as "merely natural," we will be in a better position to profit by higher forms of truth when they come our way.

Natural Problems

Another point raised by Sebastian Moore: sometimes our ordinary personal and human problems are treated in terms of the highest kind of ethical or religious crisis. Dom Sebastian points out that if all ordinary difficulties are always faced on the highest religious level as crucial problems, matters of life and death in the realm of faith and morals, we are never able to get to grips with them on our own personal level.

Suppose a person has difficulty coming to terms with some truth of faith. If this is immediately treated as a religious crisis of the highest order instead of as a personal and even psychological problem, it may be impossible to solve it. Perhaps it is not a problem at all on that religious level. It may not be a problem of sin, for example. If every problem that comes up is immediately treated in terms of sin and betrayal, our grasp of it may be totally unreal. Of course it may be a matter of sin. But let us not confuse a feeling of anxiety or insecurity with a sense of moral guilt. If we automatically assume that every little anxiety is the sign of a moral problem and then try to deal with it as a moral problem we may end up in the most awful confusion—and completely without reason. There is usually no need at all for the moral anguish we create over certain problems.

We ignore an important, psychological, natural element, which may really be the thing at issue in this particular case of this particular person. The solution of the problem may well not be in the confessional, not on a moral level, not on a religious level. It may not be a matter of faith and it may not involve one's friendship with God at all. It is quite possibly a psychological, natural, emotional problem, something that could be more easily solved on a simple, human level. Some people just can't stand having their problems on this lower level—they prefer a full-scale crisis because it makes them feel more "Christian"!

The confessor very often does not realize this. Or he may grasp it intuitively, without knowing how to tell the penitent. We may have a penitent who is bothered by this kind of problem, which is not really a moral problem and yet is an acutely anguishing problem nevertheless. He or she goes to confession with the problem and the confessor realizes that this is neither a moral nor a religious problem. So he simply dismisses it. Then the person gets extremely worried about this because for him or for her it really is a problem. That is to say, it causes an experience of real insecurity and anxiety. Now, what the priest is saying is not that this is no problem, but that it is nothing to worry about in confession. But he may brush it off as completely absurd, so that the penitent now feels guilty about having a problem. What he should really be saying is, "Look, this is not a religious problem, this is not a moral problem, and this is not a matter of sin. Your friendship with God is not involved here, and even though you may feel that it is, it isn't. This has nothing to do with your friendship with God."

What we really need to learn is how to face and handle this sort of thing on a natural level. This is a natural problem, and we have to get in touch with the natural values in ourselves that are the resources with which to meet problems like this—for instance, the resources of growing up. Problems of this kind are often problems of maturity and problems of human experience. The real trouble with many religious is that authentic human experience is side-tracked or short-circuited in the convent. One is not allowed to be an ordinary human being because one is always supposed to be living on the superhuman level. One must always be on an intense level of religious crisis or about to lose one's vocation or one's faith. As a result, some people are driven in sheer desperation to "lose their vocation" and get it over with!

But we always have to remember that all problems are illusory without some basis of natural maturity and a natural human growth. It is very important to stress these natural values. We must constantly emphasize the importance of *growing up*. Needless to say, we must not go to the other extreme and make everything an intense psychological problem. There are real religious problems which are not just psychological problems, but they may be more rare than we realize. Many religious are just not mature enough to have an authentic religious crisis!

To sum up, I would say that it is essential for us contemplatives really to hang on to the essentials of our vocation. We must face the fact that we are called to be contemplatives. If there is a real threat to our contemplative life, we must resist that threat. We must refuse to be involved in useless and foolish substitutes for the contemplative life. At the same time, we cannot possibly hang on to a dead formalistic set of pseudo-contemplative routines. The contemplative life has to be renewed and it has to be renewed *from within*. It has to be renewed by us with the help of the Holy

Spirit. This is no time for fooling around, and it is no time for being unduly influenced by the slogans of people who don't know our problems. It is possible that a great deal of the conflict that is going on in the Church today is marked by neurosis. Between the obsessive compulsive formalisms of some conservatives and the adolescent autistic thinking of some progressives! It is for us to keep our sanity if we possibly can, and to keep a certain amount of lucidity and a genuine fidelity to God's call. Let us keep alive especially the awareness of what is really authentic within our own experience, because we know, we have experienced in moments of prayer, in moments of truth and realization, what God really asks of us and what he really wishes to give us. Let us remain faithful to that truth and to that experience.

What is Monastic?

Let us now try to clear the ground for a better approach to our problems as contemplatives. The main problem is of course the renewal of the contemplative life. Our first question concerns, precisely, the term "contemplative." Should the term "contemplative religious" be used at all? There seems to be some protest about the term "monastic." I find this in a letter which I am taking as my starting point. Reference is made to a Sister who protested against the word "monastic." The Sister is quoted as saying: "I think that what I am objecting most to is the monasticism that has been imposed upon us and has become part of our structure."

Since I do not know this Sister and do not know exactly in what situation the statement was made, I cannot quite comment on it. This letter comes from a Franciscan *milieu* and the complaint against monasticism being "imposed" upon others, which is very common and in many cases a justified complaint today, usually arises in the active life and in priestly life, and even in lay life where a monastic form of spirituality has historically tended to prevail since the Middle Ages. As if sanctity for a lay person or for a secular priest consisted in living somewhat like a monk. I think perhaps it would be worth while to discuss a little what we mean by the monastic life and also, by implication, the contemplative life.

What is the best way to approach this whole question? There is no point in just giving a definition of the essence of a monk and the essence of a contemplative and so forth. Let us rather approach it from a kind of phenomenological viewpoint. This is a more modern way of looking at it. Let us consider the different kinds of aspiration and vocation which draw people to the particular life that we are leading. What induces them to seek among us something that they particularly want? What brings them here to do, together with us, something that they particularly need to do? What is it that they feel will give their life its true meaning as their personal response to God's call? In other words, let us consider the *kind of thing people have traditionally wanted to do in a cloistered life*, a life apart from the world, separated from the world.

In all religious life the postulant gets into a special relationship with civil society: a kind of relationship of opposition in some way or other with the rest of the world. This is central in all traditional forms of "dedicated life" but is most central in the so-called contemplative and cloistered orders. After all, when you talk about "cloistered life" you are defining a life (perhaps very unsatisfactorily) in terms of "separation from the world." And of course, this whole idea of separation from the world is a big problem of our time. We have to be not only separated *from* the world but also *open to* it. Let us take for granted that when we talk about separation from the world we are not talking about a fanatical hatred of the world or anything like that.

The whole question of defining our precise relation to the

world is another problem which will have to be treated somewhere else. But no matter how we look at it, when we talk about the kind of life that we have in fact embraced we are talking about a life which involves leaving the ordinary life that we knew before in order to do something else which we consider to be better because it is free from certain obstacles and hindrances. We have left our homes and families and civil life and our jobs (if we had them). We have left the university or wherever else we were. We have left our former kind of life and taken on the kind of life that we have now. Doubtless every single one of us at one time or other stopped to consider whether this was really worthwhile. Certainly one of the great problems in the religious life today is this question: Has it been worthwhile in terms of authenticity, reality, integrity, and so forth, for me to leave that other kind of life and embrace this kind of life? Is this really more real? Is this more authentic?

Very often you find people solving this question, or trying to solve it, by going from a more active kind of religious life to what we provisionally call a more contemplative life, a more cloistered and hidden kind of religious life. This assumes that one can create certain conditions which are "better" because the experience of generations has shown them to work in a certain way. We assume we can create this set of conditions and get into this new situation ourselves and thereby arrive at something very special to which we are called by God. And so in our cloistered life we try to set up conditions which make it easier and more effective to do something quite special. And what is this that we want to do? Why do we set up these conditions and do these things and what is it that we are after?

To begin with, I think that you can't say that everybody in the cloister is simply trying to do the same thing. The monastic vocation really allows quite a lot of scope for individual differences; at least it *should* allow quite a lot of

111

scope for the individual to follow a personal call, to follow something that he feels is especially relevant to him.

Historically, in the beginning of the monastic life, you find people called to a kind of special individual union with God, which they are supposed to find out about and work out for themselves after an initial period of training. The earliest model for the monastic life is that of the ascetics and virgins who lived apart from their fellow citizens in the towns of the Roman Empire, or outside the towns. These more experienced ascetics would follow their own manner of life, praying and denying themselves, and following a hidden quiet way of prayer and worship. They would receive young people who thought they were called to the same kind of thing, give them a rudimentary and individual training, and then turn them loose to carry on for themselves.

Monastic communities came only later. And these early monastic vocations were people who felt that they had an individual call to a particular kind of life. They would go off into the desert to live in a cave or somewhere, or they would take to the road and live as pilgrims and beggars.

The Franciscan way came into the Middle Ages as a salutary revolt against the highly institutionalized monastic system. St Francis made possible once again an open-ended kind of existence in which there wasn't very much predetermined for you. You were pretty free to do this or that or anything. You could be a pilgrim, you could be a hermit, and you could be a pilgrim for a while and a hermit for a while and then a scholar for a while. Then you could go to the Muslims in North Africa and get yourself martyred if you had the grace! And so forth.

The Franciscan ideal could really be regarded as a return to the authentic freedom of early monasticism. I would venture as a kind of personal guess as this point that actually the ideal of St Francis was more purely *monastic* in the true original primitive sense than the life lived by the big Benedictine and Cistercian communities of the thirteenth century where everything was so highly organized behind walls.

A Life of Charismatic Freedom

One of the essential elements of the monastic life is a kind of charismatic freedom. This seems to me to be right at the heart of this monastic vocation; and this creates a problem, of course, precisely because the monastic life as we have it is so highly organized. To what extent does this organized and disciplined and systematic life enable a person to attain a certain level of freedom interiorly in order to do what God has called him to do? To say "a life of charismatic freedom" is to speak of a life in which a person is free from certain routine cares and responsibilities and claims and demands which are regarded as less fruitful, as somewhat deadening. The monastic charism seeks to be free from these in order to be more constantly awake, alert, alive, sensitive to areas of experience which are not easily opened up in the midst of the routines which we shall call "worldly routines." On the other hand, of course, we must not develop a sort of magic idea of the contemplative life and say that when a person puts on a certain kind of habit and goes into a certain kind of cloister and lives a certain kind of rule automatically a deep inner kind of contemplative life follows. This is not necessarily so and the problem of substituting cloister routines for worldly routines can really be an evasion and a falsification of this call to authentic inner freedom. But the point is that the contemplative or monastic life is supposed to liberate a man or a woman from certain routines which are fruitless for them, although perhaps fruitful for other people, in order to let them do something else that they feel they are called to do.

I suppose here we had better say something about freedom. Here we realize that we are in trouble! We cannot possibly take these big words for granted. They call for a great deal of study, a great deal of reflection from all of us collectively and individually. It is definitely not enough to pick up some of the echoes and resonances and emotional implications of a word like freedom as it is bandied around in the religious life. These are loaded words, and they are being used in a way that can be very fruitful and very helpful, but can also be very destructive.

Freedom is also a fighting word, and we have to reflect on the reasons why. Freedom is a fighting word in the religious life today, just as it is in civil life, simply because it has been denied people so consistently and with so many fraudulent excuses. Religious have been abused in this matter like everyone else. Authority has not always been honest in its exercise. "Obedience" has been used to justify almost anything. The time has come to rectify that abuse. But as I say, we have to consider and study what freedom means, especially for us in the contemplative life.

Asceticism

Freedom for what? Obviously the traditional idea, although this has to be examined too, still holds. Traditionally in the monastic life, in the contemplative life, and in the ascetic life as a whole, there's a question of asceticism. It is understood that the freedom we seek is a freedom which is purchased at the price of renouncing another kind of freedom. The freedom that we are talking about in the contemplative life and in the monastic life is the freedom which is bought by the renunciation of licence or the simple capacity to follow any legitimate desire in any legitimate direction. Besides renouncing illegitimate freedom we also give up a certain lawful autonomy. So that we come face to face right away with the fact that the freedom we look for is bound up with restrictions. Of course, if we're going to consider contemplative freedom intelligently we must go back to the real

Trent rulings? How defensive

sources in the New Testament and especially in St Paul and
St John. I am not going to do that here. The freedom we
seek in the contemplative life is to be understood in the
light of St John's statement that the truth shall make you
free and St Paul's statement that we have the freedom of the
children of God and the freedom of the Spirit. It is also the
freedom which is not under the law. Monastic freedom does
not place its hope in the fulfillment of legal routine observances. Therefore it is very important indeed to understand
the contemplative life or the monastic life or whatever form
of life you want to call it in such a way that it does not
become a life dominated by law or a life defined by the hope
of salvation through good works. We have to take into
account the fact that Luther was a religious. They speak of
him as a "monk." He was not a monk—the Augustinians
are not monks. But Luther was a religious reacting against a
decadent religious system and returning to St Paul. Luther
wanted to "return to sources."

Whether we agree with Luther or not is another matter,
but Luther is historically important for the religious life of
the Catholic Church and for our monastic renewal. Obviously the reforms of the Council of Trent were aimed
against Luther. But now we clearly understand also that one
of the main points of Vatican II has been an implicit recognition that we are now beyond the Council of Trent. The
need for the defensive measures taken at Trent no longer
exists. We are in a totally different situation. Without aban-
doning the historic continuity which links us with the medieval past through Trent, we have to remember that the
defensive attitude taken by Trent cannot be what governs
and guides us in our religious renewal today.

To return to my point: in the contemplative and monastic
life we have sought out a certain kind of solitude and separation from the world for the sake of *freedom*.

Martha and Mary

One of the ways in which the freedom of the contemplative life is expressed is perhaps not very popular today. Still, let us consider this example of Martha and Mary. We find it in the Gospels—Martha working to provide the meal which our Lord is to eat and Mary sitting at the feet of the Lord listening to what he has to say. Martha complains that Mary does not help her, and Jesus defends Mary, saying: "Martha, you are solicitous, you are disturbed with many things! Mary has chosen the best part and it shall not be taken from her."

Traditionally this has been explained by the Fathers of the Church, in a way that we all well know, to justify a certain renunciation of good, productive, healthy social activity in order simply to listen to the words of Christ, to be silent and listen to God. Of course this really doesn't solve any problems, yet the use of this text as a justification of the contemplative life does rest on a solid psychological basis, on a basis of real experience which can be verified in the lives of those who have tried to put it into practice and know what it means.

When someone has an authentic call to the contemplative life or to the monastic life, that call can be understood in terms of this Gospel text and experienced in the way that is suggested by it. Our vocation can be understood as the resolution of a conflict which is expressed in this story, a conflict in ourselves. Now the important thing is that the conflict *is in ourselves* rather than projected outward into *institutions*. It is one thing to experience in our own lives the difference between the action of Martha and the listening of Mary—but quite another to "prove" that Trappists are "better" than Dominicans!

The fact that this conflict between Martha and Mary became an institutional matter in the thirteenth century does not concern us here, it simply obscures the issue. Ever since that time, there has been a great deal of argument about the respective value of active Orders and contemplative Orders. This is no longer to the point. Where the conflict resolves itself is in our own hearts as individual persons or small groups, called to this particular life of quiet, of *freedom to listen* to the Word of God in our hearts. We experience in ourselves a new and special kind of truth when we imitate Mary. We who have this particular call recognize that when we are agitated by all kinds of external concerns which do not touch us deeply at all we are less authentic, less real, less ourselves, less what we are supposed to be. We feel less faithful to the will of God than when we remain simply in an attitude of freedom and attentiveness to his word, his love, and his will. This Gospel text illustrates our experience that we are summoned by the Holy Spirit to make *an act of preference.* We are called to prefer the apparent uselessness, the apparent unproductiveness, the apparent inactivity of simply sitting at the feet of Jesus and listening to him. We are called to prefer this over an apparently more productive, more active, more busy life. We quietly affirm that there is something more important than "getting things done."

Together with this is another implied assumption: that this preference goes against the ideas of the majority of our fellow human beings at any given moment and especially today in the twentieth century. Our act of preference for "quiet" is at the same time an implicit protest and defiance, a protest against and a defiance of the counter opinion of those who are absolutely convinced that our life is useless and who reproach us for it.

Here we find another piece in the jigsaw puzzle that we are putting together. A very important piece is this element of preferring to be at the feet of Jesus and to listen to him in secret, even though we can't fully explain it to other people. Other people are not going to understand it. Other good people are not going to understand it, other Christians and other Catholics. We realize all this and we make our choice anyhow. In this contemplative life of ours, in our monastic existence, we are going against the stream.

The Discipline of Listening

This puts us in a very uncomfortable position. We realize that if we get excited about those who criticize us and devote too much effort to answering them, we become solicitous and are drawn away from the listening which we are called to cultivate as a special kind of discipline. This brings us to another point in this Martha-Mary picture that we are considering. It is an obscure realization which is never emphasized enough. Just remaining quietly in the presence of God, listening to him, being attentive to him, requires a lot of courage and know-how. This discipline of listening and of attention is a very high form of ascetic discipline, a rather difficult one to maintain. In fact, there are lots of people who do not have the strength nor the grace to maintain this kind of discipline for very long. Doubtless when a person is clearly not able to do this, maybe he shouldn't try. Our asceticism will consist in discovering to what extent each one of us can simply remain quiet in passive attention to God, and to what extent we do need some activity, some work that does not completely interfere with this but which relaxes us and takes us away from mere concentration. We all need a certain amount of activity that enables us to participate healthily in the life of our community. We need work that keeps us in tune physically and psychologically so that we are able to listen fruitfully instead of just going stale and turning off completely. There is such a thing as overdoing interior prayer and overdoing concentration and overdoing recollection. This can be harmful. It only deadens our capacity to listen and to attend to God.

This we all know. But let us emphasize the fact that our attention to Jesus alone, our listening to his word, our attitude of interior conviction, is something we come to experience as the highest value in our life. Contemplatives are people who experience this. This is in itself a most effective discipline and a most purifying form of ascetic training and formation. In this tranquil, empty, peaceful solitude a person receives quietly, hiddenly and secretly from God a great deal of benefit, simply by listening and quiet attention.

In this connection let me refer to a passage by St John of the Cross. Speaking of solitude and the benefits of solitude on the soul, and the tranquil listening to God which he calls the "tranquillity of solitude in which the soul is moved and guided to find things by the spirit of God," he says that in this solitude, in this listening, in this tranquil attention to God, God acts directly upon the one who prays, doing it by himself, communicating himself to the soul, without other means, without passing through angels, men, images or forms. He adds that in this solitude, God and the beloved are together in great intimacy: "The solitude wherein the soul lives before time was the desire to be without all the blessings of the world for the sake of love."

Now, that is a good definition, or a good indication of something of that choice that I was speaking of—a desire, an active desire to forgo the benefits, privileges, blessings, advantages which are characteristic of a worldly life or an active life. Characteristic, incidentally, of a good worldly life. We do not deny the goodness of all these things but we renounce their goodness for something else which we see to be better for us, but which does not appear at all to anybody else.

Even at the very beginning of a contemplative life, when a person has received this call from God, he does realize obscurely that for him the supreme value of life is going to consist in a surrender directly to God, in the hope and confidence and belief that God will act directly upon him without the intermediary of ordinary active human ideas or agencies. Of course it may be normal and may be fruitful and sanctifying for most people to reach God through the medium of married love and by bringing up children in an active life, and many may find God better in an active apostolic life fully mixed up with the things of time and of the world. This may be a perfectly normal and perhaps in some respects a better way. Certainly it is a way that the rest of the human race appreciates more. Nevertheless, there is for us this mysterious call to a life of direct communion with and dependence upon and guidance by and formation by and purification by God in silence, in prayer, in solitude, in detachment, in freedom.

It is here that we have to seek the real meaning of freedom in the contemplative life. We renounce other forms of freedom in order to have this kind of freedom. Therefore it becomes necessary to accept restrictions, restraints, self-denial, sacrifice, and so forth, as we have always heard and always known. But it is much deeper than we have always heard. Restriction and sacrifice have to be accepted in order that this inner freedom may grow. Therefore in the contemplative life, in the monastic life, there is necessarily an element of renouncing advantages, renouncing even certain fruitful activities which sanctify people in other vocations, in order to find our expansion and development and rest and peace in a totally different dimension. For a great deal of the time this solitude and listening are painful, difficult, full of hardship, and very demanding. The contemplative life is especially demanding because we are alone and unable to explain ourselves to other people. Admittedly this is very hazardous. So many people are not able to handle this isolation, as we know from experience. They crack up! Perhaps we can say that in our life there are many people who do have an authentic appreciation of what this *might be* for them and yet they are not able to attain to it. We must not blame them. We must not say that it is their fault. We must not say that they have not been generous enough. It is just a fact that few people are able to live in this solitary "desert" for a lifetime. Those of us who recognize ourselves really called to this should be very happy—much more happy than we usually are about it. We should be very grateful to God that he called us to this life and that he has called us to this particular kind of peace in this particular kind of fulfillment, which in so many respects is an unfulfillment and which is almost scandalous to people of our time, so intent upon human fulfillment. Yet even they, when they come in contact with people who have lived in a solitary or clositered life, recognize that there is a special kind of happiness in this life.

Contemplative and Mystic

Let us finally consider the question of using the word "contemplative" for all this. This word, contemplative, is another one that calls for a great deal of reflection and study on our part. There are many problems. First of all, the term "contemplative" is ambiguous. In the debates that were carried on rather hotly in the 1920s between the Jesuits and the Dominicans in France about the mystical life, mystical graces, and contemplative life, the term "contemplative" tended to be used as it had been used for several centuries before with overtones of *mysticism*. Indeed, very often you find that the word "contemplative" is a safer, vaguer, broader and more discreet word for "mystic." "Mystic" seems to be a more scary word than "contemplative." People hesitate to use it. Also "mystic" tends to suggest women with stigmata and people having visions, or people who have manifestly attained to mystical union in an extraordinary way. As I understand it from having read a lot of the literature on the subject, the word "contemplative" has been rather widely used as a discreet term for persons enjoying a certain low grade of mystical grace that has nothing to do with visions

121

and has nothing to do with anything very special, but corresponds to a kind of quiet, unitive, and passive absorption in God. This is definitely a special grace of God which is much more widespread than is usually realized. It is really accessible to lots of people. Doubtless many who receive it cannot stay with it for very long but nevertheless it is a sort of borderline mystical state.

Now, this use of "contemplation" can be very misleading because if you say we are a "contemplative Order," we are a "contemplative community," this is a "contemplative cloister," are you intimating that everybody in the cloister is a mystic of this particular kind? Or that everybody in the cloister *should be* a mystic of this particular kind? The answer is obviously "No"! Nor is anyone asserting that contemplatives in this sense are found only in cloisters. They are found rather widely outside cloisters. There are plenty of housewives with noisy children and all kinds of duties who are leading a contemplative life in this sense. And there are plenty of people teaching in universities or engaged in intellectual life in one form or other who are or can be contemplatives in this sense without very much difficulty.

It is not even necessarily true that life in a contemplative cloister is more propitious to this unitive way of prayer than any other kind of life. It should be, it's designed for that. We have to admit this when we speak of Carmelite cloisters. Obviously St Teresa meant Carmel to be a place where this kind of contemplative prayer, quasi-mystical prayer, near-mystical prayer, should be not unusual. But nevertheless, we all know from experience that there are lots of people in monasteries and cloisters who do not respond to this kind of thing at all, who are mystified by it or scared by it or upset by it or disturbed by it, and who nevertheless can do very well indeed in a life of service, charity, and devotion. This brings us to the important point that the essential of our life is not precisely or chiefly that it disposes us for contemplation in the sense that I have just described but that it produces *a community in which the Spirit can speak to us all in different ways.* The longing for a real evangelical community life is certainly as strong today, above all in the young people who are coming to religious life.

Christian Community

There's nothing wrong whatever in dropping the use of this word "contemplation" completely if we want to look at the whole thing from a different point of view and use a different language—the language of the last chapters of St John's Gospel, for example. Here the mystical theology, so to speak, of the New Testament is fully exposed in the context of the Last Supper; that is to say, in the ideal, perfect expression of Christian community. And so suppose that the term "contemplation" is unsatisfactory—suppose there are lots of people who are mystified and put off when we express the idea of union with God and direct communion with him in the language of "contemplation." If this insistence on "contemplation" becomes scandalous and difficult for them let us re-formulate it in terms of the New Testament. Let us think of it in terms of knowing Jesus, being one of his disciples, being a member of the loving community which is called together in his merciful love, called to share his body and his blood together around the table of the Eucharistic banquet, called to realize in our love for one another and in our love for Jesus his presence in us. Let us consider the fourteenth chapter of St John, for example, as an expression of the experience of Jesus present to us in our communal life, in the quiet of that cenacle which we have chosen and which is our cloister.

> Do not let your hearts be troubled. Trust in God still and trust in me. There are many rooms in my Father's house. If there were not, I should have told you. I am going now to prepare a place for you and after I have

gone and prepared you a place, I shall return to take you with me. So that where I am, you may be too. You know the way and the place where I am going. Thomas said, Lord, we do not know where you are going so how can we know the way? Jesus said, I am the way, the truth, and the light. No one can come to the Father except through me. If you know me, you know my Father too. From this moment, you know him and have seen him.

Our life in our cloistered community is a life in which we should have access to many mansions. Let us always remember that. That should be a kind of *magna carta* of the monastic life. "There are many mansions in my Father's house." Here is a place where we are gathered together, called out of the world in the sense that the disciples were called there to the cenacle with Jesus. Like the disciples we are waiting for him to come and bring us to the place that he has prepared for us. This is the language of the New Testament. This may appeal more to some than the language of "contemplation" but it comes basically down to the same thing, the same experience, Mary's love and total trust in the Lord who promises to manifest his glory to us and in us through the Church.

In this life of waiting and of trusting, of attending entirely to Jesus' will for us and to his love for us living in simplicity with the brothers and the sisters, in the breaking of bread and in mutual love, we learn gradually to experience a new dimension of our Christian life. We come to see not only that we are going somewhere but that we have already arrived, and that Jesus is the way and the truth and the life. He is the beginning and the end; to live in him is to be not only on the way but at the end, to have arrived.

Our life in Christ is all-sufficient. What we have been calling the "contemplative life" is a life of awareness that one thing is necessary, that Jesus is alone necessary and that to live for him and in him is all-sufficient. To live in him pacifies everything. To live in him takes care of everything. To live in him answers all questions even though we don't quite understand or hear the answers.

So when Philip says to him, as we do, "Show us the Father," Jesus replies (and this is our life), "To have seen me is to have seen the Father, so how can you say, let us see the Father? Do you not believe that I am in the Father and that the Father is in me? It is the Father living in me who is doing this work."

This we have to believe in our own life. If we are living in Christ, we are, so to speak, face to face with the Father but we do not know it and we cannot see him. We have to be content to be face to face with him in a way that we cannot understand or see. But we must realize that Jesus working in us is carrying out the Father's work and manifesting the Father to us:

> It is to the glory of my Father that you should bear much fruit and then you will be my disciples. As the Father has loved me, so I have loved you. Remain in my love. If you keep my commandments you will remain in my love, just as I have kept my Father's commandments and remained in his love. I have told you this so that my joy may be in you and your joy may be complete. This is my commandment, love one another as I have loved you. A man can have no greater love than to lay down his life for his friend. I call you friends because I have made known to you everything I have learned from my Father. You did not choose me. No, I chose you and I commissioned you to go out and bear fruit, fruit that will last; and then the Father will give you anything that you ask him in my name. What I command you is to love one another.

Built into all this passage of St John is the basic idea that if we live by Christ's love in the Christian community, we will experience, obscurely, in some way, what it means that Christ is sent to us from the Father and dwells in us by his

Spirit, fulfilling in us the will of the Father, so that what we experience in our communal Christian life is what it means to be united to God in Christ and to be children of God in his Spirit.

We have now considered two aspects of our life, one the more personal, solitary one, and the other more communal one. We have emphasized the fact that these are two aspects of the same thing. We do not need to know which one of these is right because they are both right. What we really have to discover for ourselves and for our communities is how to reach the right kind of combination of these two elements so that each one of us will be able to live fully the kind of vocation to which he or she has been called.

Active Service

The word "contemplative" is used both juridically and mystically, and this creates confusion. The term "contemplative life" has become a kind of juridical term synonymous with "cloistered life," and yet it also has mystical overtones. Now, you cannot really have such a thing as a *contemplative institution*. Contemplation simply cannot be institutionalized. In fact you can create a cloistered life with certain laws and regulations, and inside this cloistered life there may be some people who are really called to be contemplatives in the sense of mystics of a very simple kind. There may be other people, perhaps the majority, whose whole life is centred on a kind of simple active service and worship within the cloister, without a thought of mystical prayer. And this is a very special, very real kind of vocation. It emphatically does not want to become involved in active external concerns, and does want simply to lead a quiet, well-ordered life in the cloister, centred principally on liturgical worship, on manual work, simple service, and communal life and fraternal charity.

What we have to do at this present point in our study is to

realize that when the law talks of the contemplative life it is really thinking of this second class of people, interested more in active service in the cloister than in simple contemplative prayer. Now, it would be a great mistake to oppose these two to each other, because in fact a person who is called to be a contemplative in the cloister is going to be greatly helped toward that end by living the simple life of service we have been talking about. Also, those who live a life of cloistered service and liturgical prayer, with a certain amount of meditation with reading, will come very close to a kind of simple contemplative peace in their hearts, which, however, they will experience in a slightly different way. It may be a sense of peace from having done their duty—the peace that comes from living an ordered life, a quiet industrious life of devotion and consecration. Perhaps this simple and active, dutiful and devout peace is what most cloistered religious seek

The opposition between the two kinds of approach can be exaggerated, and cause an unfortunate split in the community. To some extent this is due, I think, to the fact that the active service people lack imagination. They seem to feel that we who have emphasized solitude and contemplation are somehow running them down. There is a kind of "chip on the shoulder" attitude on the part of the active service types—they resent the claims of the more contemplative members of the community, as if on the one hand we claim superiority, and on the other are trying to get out of work. So we notice a kind of defensive attitude on the part of some in our monasteries, who are good people and work hard. They get a lot of satisfaction out of work, which is fine; but they feel that the "Marys" are shirking their responsibility and are not realistic. They seem to think the "contemplatives" are deceiving themselves and just sitting around twiddling their thumbs in a state of quietism and inertia.

There has been a certain amount of tension between the two groups on this account and so contemplation, even in the so-called contemplative monasteries, tends always to be in disrepute. Even so-called contemplatives can look upon contemplation as something unrealistic, as if the real point of monastic life were only active cloistered service. Perhaps it is—I'm not coming to any conclusions on this now. I am just sorting out the different manifestations of these two tendencies. Many so-called contemplatives are simply called to a kind of cloistered service, and it is therefore unfortunate that the life should be officially called contemplative, because the use of the term is ambiguous for these people and causes a lot of doubt and confusion. In practice they solve it by saying that liturgy is contemplation, and he who is zealous about going to choir on time is a "true contemplative."

Attentiveness to God

I am now talking more particularly to those who really seek a deeper experience of God, a deeper expansion of the religious consciousness, a deeper understanding and knowledge of the things of God through love. A moment ago I described two approaches to the life of Mary, the life of sitting at the feet of Christ. The life of Mary can be seen as a life of solitary listening, solitary attentiveness, interior purification, interior disposability, openness, readiness to be spoken to, an interior sensitivity, an interior awareness, all of which we cultivate in prayer. A person called to this kind of contemplation will quite spontaneously seek more time to be alone, quiet, simply listening to God.

Of course where people go wrong is that they fail to realize that this simple prayer can go on even though one may be at work. This state of attention to God certainly can coexist with a simple kind of action, and the fact that one is not aware of attending to God is perhaps better. It is not necessarily the best and most healthy thing for a person to be sitting quietly, intensely aware of himself as passive. It is better for a person to be somewhat active and not to be aware that anything special is going on, provided that there is no absorption in anything else.

Take the activity of sweeping the floor or washing dishes or chopping wood or cutting grass or something like that. These activities are not distracting. We do not become absorbed in them and it is quite possible to engage in them without any sense that we are praying or that we are doing anything other than simply doing what we do in such a way that we remain quietly close to God. Now, the point I am trying to get to is this: what this attentiveness to God really means is not just a particular psychological state or a peculiar kind of recollection, but it is part and parcel of the experience of love in everyday life. Consequently love is the thing that really creates unity in the apparent division between the Marthas and the Marys of the cloister. It also creates unity in ourselves—and unites us *with reality*. Maybe the Marthas obscurely realize that when they are giving their bodies and their senses something neutral to do they are at peace and somehow or another united with God, without realizing it or experiencing anything special. They may find that when they sit down and do nothing and simply try to attend to God in a recollected state they become tense and confused, too aware of themselves. The other people, the contemplatives and the Marys, so to speak, are able to do this and enjoy listening to God and they think perhaps they are better off that way. In actual fact, what happens is that the Marys also enter into great dryness and do not necessarily enjoy or get much sweetness out of this attentiveness to God. But they have to go on with it anyway because they cannot help themselves.

They are called and drawn to this in such a way that they realize that the greatest benefit in their life is going to come from this simple peaceful attentiveness to God even though it is arid and quiet and dry. And they too will learn, as I said, to combine it with simple tasks and manual work. It is also a good thing to be involved in some work that takes your mind off prayer completely, that rests the mind and gives it a change. The mind is not rested by falling into complete inactivity but by varying its activity. This variety is important.

The essential thing in our life is this fact that it be centred on love as sufficient unto itself. Love alone is enough, regardless of whether it produces anything. It is better for love not to be especially oriented to results, to a work to be done, a class to be taught, people to be taken care of in the hospital, or anything like that. In the active life love is channelled into something that gets results. In the so-called contemplative life love is sufficient unto itself. It does of course work, it does do things, but in our life the emphasis is on love above everything else, on faith above everything else. Especially on faith above works! The characteristic of our life is that it makes us realize more deeply how much we depend directly on God by faith, how much we depend directly on the mercy of God, how much we depend upon receiving everything directly from him and not through the mediation of our own activity. While we continue to act, we act in such a way that this consciousness of dependence on God is greater, more continual, more all-embracing and more satisfactory than it is in the active life. It is in this that we find our peace. It is in this that we find our whole meaning for existence. What is called the contemplative life is really a life arranged in such a way that a person can more easily and more simply and more naturally live in an awareness of direct dependence on God—almost with the sense of realizing consciously, at every moment, how much we depend on God; and receive from him directly everything that comes to us as a pure gift; and experience, taste in our hearts, the love of God in this gift, the delicacy and the personal attention of God to us in his merciful love, which St Thérèse of Lisieux brought out so beautifully.

This is of course true to some extent of all religious life. But in other forms of religious life the emphasis tends to be outgoing, centred on what we are doing and on the results we are getting and on the relationships we are setting up with other people; whereas in our life, the so-called contemplative life, the emphasis is on our direct relationship to God and our experience with that relationship, that experience of spiritual childhood, sonship in the Spirit. We cultivate a sense of direct dependence on God and look to God in order to receive all from him at every moment.

And this life takes two forms, as I say. Some see it more in terms of a simple service in the cloister, liturgical prayer, and active work around the house. Others see it more in terms of solitary meditation and direct listening. But the contrast between these two should not be exaggerated; they're really doing pretty much the same thing and they should feel that they are sisters to one another like Martha and Mary. For the medieval writers always ended up by saying that Martha and Mary complete each other and that no community would be a full monastic community if there were not Marthas and Marys together. They are both needed, and the real community is a synthesis of these two aspects of the one monastic life.

Deviations

At this point it might be well to pause and consider the fact that in both these approaches to the hidden life of prayer, the cloistered life, there can be and often are, as we know by experience, deviations and wrong directions. Many people misunderstand both these ways of approaching our life with God, the way of cloistered service and the way of solitary meditative absorption and prayer and listening. Now, the problem is in each case to ensure a genuine, living, healthy occupation with God that is based on faith, on real living faith and also on common sense. We must cultivate a realistic and healthy view of human life. It is easy to live *inhumanly* in a cloister, to cultivate a sort of fanatical and compulsive addiction to the practices of cloistered life. Instead of living our lives in a healthy, productive, normal, humble, quiet, matter-of-fact sort of way, on a basis of deep faith, we may get tense and over-preoccupied, over-anxious, almost superstitious and fanatical about the things that we are doing. The more active people whose life is centred on cloistered service tend to develop a kind of scrupulosity, a kind of obsession with doing everything the right way—they become obsessed with the idea that there is only one right way to do it and that's the way it's going to be done by everybody! They are obsessed with what they are doing and in seeing that it is recognized as right by others. In other words, they develop an excessive preoccupation with themselves.

The same thing happens in a different way with the person who tends to prefer a silent, solitary, meditative approach. By way of brief and shorthand identification, I would say that what we are concerned with is people who become unconsciously centred on themselves rather than on God. We find that they develop a kind of cult of themselves, a cult of their own works, their own personality and their own activities. They are engrossed in their own prayers and their own feelings and their own experiences, instead of the cult of God. They're not worhipping God, really. They become, as it were, hypnotized by themselves. And they can do this sometimes with the best will in the world. They can rationalize all this very cleverly as service of God and it can become really a complicated business, this sort of fanatical involvement in oneself, justified by rationalization in which everything is theoretically ordered to God.

So there are people who are intensely involved in themselves, all tied up in themselves, and rather unpleasant to live with because of this. They take it out in various subtle ways on other people. They justify all this by appealing to God, to faith and to religion. Sometimes passive meditating people are extremely aware of every little thing that disturbs them, and become extremely critical of anything that interferes with their absorption in the experience of sweetness that they are having. This is, generally speaking, a sign that there is something wrong somewhere, that the contemplative thing isn't quite as authentic as it appears to be. It is more centred on one's own self than it is on God.

In all cases, we have to remember the basic importance of a good, common-sense, realistic, human view of life; and where this common-sense, human realism is not found it must be cultivated. If it cannot be cultivated, then there is something definitely wrong with that person's vocation. But of course there will always be people who have been to some extent wounded, twisted, and injured by the inhumanity of an abstract kind of life. They will be semi-neurotics, who nevertheless get along in the cloister. They can remain in the cloister. They can be lived with and helped. They can even be of real positive value to the community in spite of their shortcomings. I suppose we could say that in a certain way we are all slightly nuts. We are all a little bit crazy and we all have to get along with one another in spite of our little eccentricities and quirks of character. There is evidently a little bit of the neurotic in almost everybody today. This has to be understood and accepted. Anyway, the great thing is to maintain a healthy atmosphere.

The basic requirement of the contemplative and cloistered life today is this: before all else, before we indulge in asceticism or go on to quiet contemplative absorption in God, we must recognize the need to maintain a healthy human atmosphere and a normal human relationship to one another and to reality in our communities.

This, of course, goes without saying, but it cannot be over-emphasized; it's so easily forgotten. People become so tied up in abstract ascetic or contemplative projects, things that they think they ought to do, that they forget the basic reality of living as human beings first of all. We have to be, first of all, healthy, mature, honest, objective, humble men and women before we can go on to be ascetics and mystics and contemplatives. This must never be forgotten and it has to be continually returned to because it is the foundation on which all the rest is built.

Penance

Now let us take up another very important aspect of the contemplative life. In so far as it is a life of freedom it has to be a life of penance. This may sound contradictory to those who take only a superficial view of freedom, but when we realize the true depth of the Christian idea of freedom we realize that it is essentially bound up with penance. What our life is supposed to do for us is to guarantee us a certain freedom of spirit. The true freedom of spirit that St Paul and St John speak of is the *truth* that makes us free. The monastic life seeks to provide a certain kind of truth by a really authentic penance. One of the things necessary today in the renewal of our religious life and our contemplative life is the renewal of the spirit of penance. But it has to be a *renewal,* not a return to a concept of strictness which has prevailed for the last two or three hundred years. True penance is more than legalistic strictness, a fanatical, obsessive, and compulsive sort of strictness about keeping small and rather arbitrary rules, just for their own sake. Let us face the fact right away, that this unsatisfactory concept of penance, while it had a value at a certain time, is much too limited and much too rigid. It has to a great extent lost all meaning to people in our time, whether for better or for worse. I won't go into the discussion of whether this shows that the people of our time are better or worse than people of other times. But the fact remains, that the kind of penitential discipline presupposed by a series of formal and rigid little observances has ceased to have any meaning to modern people.

A person who had bought this concept of life felt that in doing all these things he was being a real "penitent" and "denying himself." And yet they were comparatively easy to do. It was to some extent simply an act, playing a penitential role. Of course it was not all that easy. Some of the penitential things were really a hardship. For example, the old rules about clothing when you had to sleep in all your habit even in the hottest nights of summer. There was all the paraphernalia of the old habit with the rather complicated and heavy underwear we used to have. You really were hot in that dormitory cell, sleeping in all those clothes! You knew that it was summer! That was a trying and exacting and difficult thing to do and it required a lot of resolution and a lot of prayer! It meant a certain amount of anguish— the business of having prickly heat all summer long with no relief possible from it. You just couldn't get away from prickly heat because you just never stopped sweating and there was no way to be dry for more than ten seconds. You just never dried out.

Well, without going on with this, you can see that this refinement of discipline in matters of petty regulations is no longer adequate as a Christian idea of penance even though it may be difficult, even though it may be demanding. This is not the right approach. Experience has taught us that this simply no longer really works. We still have in our communities many excellent people who have been formed by this kind of practice and we admire these people very much; but we also have people who have been broken and twisted and distorted by this kind of practice. We instinctively feel that they did not come to the cloister just to be deformed in this particular kind of way, and therefore this dehumanizing concept of penance is insufficient. It does not come near the demand of the New Testament idea of penance. The distinction is this: the old idea of penance that I've been talking about is a limited one, very demanding within a small area but not really going very deep. It is external, and, in a certain sense, it's easier—it's kind of an evasion of the real penance of giving up ourselves. Is it real self-sacrifice or is it only will-training? It may be purifying up to a point but it leaves intact the inmost ego, and a person can be really strict in this kind of penance and remain very proud and harsh and extremely uncharitable. A cruel, aggressive and vindictive kind of person can flourish on this kind of penance. Real penance is aimed at the deep root of pride and the deep root of uncharitableness. Real penance aims at that vindictiveness and that persecuting mentality which so many of these strict people developed in the past.

But we must not go to the other extreme. That we now in the monastic life or the cloistered life or the contemplative life are simply throwing away all these practices and living in a kind of freedom of spirit without any real discipline is fatal. There is no hope of any good coming out of this. It will only destroy monasticism. The freedom that we are looking for must never be considered a kind of mere spontaneous following of natural tendencies, innocent natural feelings, and so forth. This idea of mere personal fulfillment, a more or less natural fulfillment of spontaneous good instincts and desires, is not good enough. If there is real charity present, if you have real honest-to-goodness community relationships in which there is real love, certainly this will do an enormous amount—but you can't have this without real self-denial, and the problem is, of course, to what extent real love is found in these relationships which are sought for and pointed to as the solution. To what extent are they really love, and to what extent are they mere gregariousness, vapid togetherness? We cannot be content with a superficial chumminess and euphoria, the kind of cheerfulness that depends on having a good time. We have been at this kind of thing for a couple of years and I think we are beginning to see the insufficiency of a community life in which there is a great deal of chumminess and a certain amount of openness and also a lot of confusion. Community means more than people propping each other up in a desperate kind of way. It means more than interminable talking and interminable wandering around looking for something that brings joy. This is not going to do the trick.

Basically there is only one Christian freedom, which is the freedom of the cross. It is the freedom that comes for one who has completely given himself with Christ on the cross, has risen with Christ and has his freedom—not simply in ordinary human spontaneity but in the spontaneity of the Spirit of God, who is given to us in exchange for our own spirit when and if we die on the cross with Christ. The pattern of the monastic life is a real death and resurrection, and for us especially there is this element of a real death to the world, to the ordinary life that we would otherwise be living as Christians or as active apostles. Whatever we call our life, cloistered or contemplative or monastic, it does imply a real break and therefore a real liberation, by a kind of death, from the claims and demands of a highly distracted and confused life in the world; although this, of course, may have a few Christian dimensions of its own. It might even be more Christian than our life. In certain circumstances it might be, but the fact remains that in response to the call of God we have made this real break and sought this real liberation from the whole network of needs, servitudes and demands which secular life imposes on people. There is no real freedom in our life without this death and resurrection—without this clean break.

Our freedom is by no means simply a removal of obstacles which permits us to fulfill our best natural aspirations. That has to be perfectly clear. We do not come to the cloister simply to become artists or to become musicians or to make friends with other people. We do not come to the cloister for the expansion of a merely human existence, because that can be done much better somewhere else. The real expansion of human existence in that kind of dimension is to be sought in married life. We do not come to the cloister to find the same kind of fulfillment and expansion of our human character and personality as we would find in marriage or in a creative secular existence, a professional career in the world. We come here for a specific and precise aim, which is a special kind of transformation in Christ and a special kind of transformation in the Spirit. The root of our penance is not at all just the embracing of ascetical routine. We come here for transformation, to be transformed not by simple convent discipline or by monastic ascetic practices. We come here to be transformed by the Spirit. We do not bring to the cloister or to the solitude of the monastery or the woods simply our own personality and our own aspirations plus a set of ascetic tools that we're going to work with to make ourselves more perfect. The idea that one remains essentially oneself and in command of oneself, and simply uses ascetic techniques to become more perfect, is essentially misleading. It leads to a wrong concept of penance, which is really no penance at all. It is mere wilful rigidity without any transformation.

We come to the cloister to surrender ourselves to Christ and to his Spirit in a kind of death, in order to live again in a life which he gives us. The freedom that we seek in the cloister is the freedom to be open to the new life which comes from Christ, the freedom to follow his Spirit. We seek a virginal freedom to follow the bridegroom wherever he goes, to be attentive to his every inspiration and to listen to the personal message that he has for us. This can come to us from no other source except from him speaking in our hearts. The institution of a certain kind of strict cloistered and solitary life is aimed precisely to protect this inner atmosphere of silence, listening, and freedom in which Christ can do in us the work he wishes to do.

The root of our penance is faith. The root of our life of *metanoia* is a real faith in Christ, a real faith in our vocation, a real faith in the transforming power of the cross, a faith in God's promises, a faith that if we give up ourselves and our ambitions, even our spiritual ambitions, if we deliver ourselves utterly and totally into the hands of Christ and to his love, we will indeed be transformed in his time, in his way, by his Spirit. Not in our time, not in our way, and not by our own spirit.

We do not come here to be transformed by our own will and our own spirit. We come here to make this complete surrender in faith. Whether we go by the old way or by the new way, this faith is radically and urgently and critically the most important thing. This is what we have to cultivate and this is what we have, above all, to pray for.

Prayer for Faith

So I would say, the root of renewal for our life implies renewal in the spheres of prayer and of penance. We do not yet know exactly in what this renewal will consist. These are the things that we have to discover collectively and individually by a real cooperative search under the guidance of the Holy Spirit. But the root of it all for all of us is prayer for faith. We must pray to the Lord at every moment to increase our faith because the root of renewal is faith. In proportion as we grow in faith, we keep closer and closer to him who has called us. In proportion as our faith develops it gives us the vision by which we can see our errors, and we can see the wrong road, instinctively. By our faith we will come to a closer union with Christ, a deeper dependence on him so that he will be able to guide us through the difficulties, the obstacles, the confusions and the errors that we are likely to meet in this way of renewal. So prayer for faith is absolutely the most fundamental thing and we must not forget how great is the power of God to give us what we need and in the most surprising ways. For example, I just had a letter from a person who claimed that she had been an atheist for quite some time. She is a young married woman, evidently baptised a Catholic in childhood and brought up perhaps as a Catholic. She could see no logical reason for the existence of God. People had been trying to prove to her the existence of God and it made no impression on her whatever. All this had no meaning whatever to her and she simply could not believe in God. Until all of a sudden one day, instead of arguing with her, some priest said, "Look, God wants your heart, not your mind: God loves you." All of a sudden this whole thing collapsed and there broke through into her heart the sense of who God really is and what he really meant to her. She saw how desperately she needed this God who loved her, who was calling her to accept his love and to love him in return. The whole reality of the thing just simply burst through, whereas arguments about the existence of God and intellectual discussion of God and so forth had meant nothing. So it is with us. We get so involved in all these intellectual and abstract discussions that we forget the basic—this call of God's love to us, urging us to love him in return and to open our hearts to him and to give him our hearts so that he may fill them with love and faith. So let us then do this. Let us pray for faith, let us pray for an increase of faith and give ourselves, totally, completely, and with perfect confidence to the God who loves us and calls us to his love.

In closing, let me quote a sentence from Clement of Alexandria which I just happened to turn up in some notes here.

Comparing the Christian to Ulysses on his ship as he travelled in his journey homeward, he speaks of how Ulysses escaped the lure of the sirens by being tied to the mast of his vessel. This has traditionally been a kind of image of the soul resisting the allurements of what does not really concern it. Clement of Alexandria compares the Christian to Ulysses bound to the mast. It is a good image of our life and its restrictions. He says:

> Bound to the wood of a cross, thou art free from all danger of destruction. God's *Logos* will steer thy ship and the Holy *Pneuma* or the Holy Spirit will give thee a safe return to heaven's harbour.

So let us consider our own lives in the light of this image, and, trusting God, remain bound to the wood of the cross; so that dying with Christ and rising with him we may be brought to union with him forever in heaven by his Holy Spirit.

THE WISDOM OF THE DESERT

"What can we gain by sailing to the moon if we are not able to cross the abyss that separates us from ourselves?" So asked Thomas Merton in his Introduction to this classic collection of "sayings" of the Desert Fathers, and his words are as relevant today as when they were first written.

In his translation of "apothegms" written by and about the Desert Fathers we meet SS Antony the Great, Pachomius, Moses, and a host of other colourful "Abbas". The sayings are dry, laconic, and often salted with an offbeat wit similar to the Zen Buddhist *koans* which so impressed Merton toward the end of his life. They are full of an honesty and simplicity that ring strikingly fresh in a society fed on the platitudes of politicians and the mass media. They are "soundbites" with bite.

This edition has been expanded with the inclusion of Merton's essay on Clement of Alexandria, not a Desert Father himself but one of their chief inspirations, followed by his translation of selections from Clement's *Protreptikos* (the "persuasion"). This philosophical masterpiece, addressed to cultured Greek pagans, ranges from acute social satire to lofty religious contemplation, and can speak to our own age as it did to the Desert Fathers. This has never previously been commercially published.

A final section is provided by Merton's essay on "The Spiritual Father in the Desert Tradition," expanding on the special role of the "Abba."

THE WAY OF CHUANG-TZU

Merton described this, his personal favourite of his books, as "not attempts at faithful reproduction but ventures in personal and spiritual interpretation." As free, interpretative readings, they are very much Merton's own, the result of five years of reading, study and meditation.

Chuang Tzu, the most spiritual of the classic Chinese philosophers, is the chief historical spokesman for Taoism. Through his writings and those of other Taoist sages, Indian Buddhism was transformed in China into what we now know by its Japanese name—Zen.

The Chinese sage abounds in wit, paradox, satire and shattering insight into the true ground of being. Merton here brings a vivid, modern idiom to the timeless wisdom of Tao.

THOUGHTS ON THE EAST

The Eastern religious traditions, especially the varieties of Buddhism, were the last great passion in Thomas Merton's life. His participation in a monastic conference in Asia led to his premature, accidental death. He discoursed on equal terms with the Dalai Lama, and extracts from their interviews appear in this book.

George Woodcock, author of the highly acclaimed *Thomas Merton: Monk and Poet*, completed the introduction to this collection shortly before his own death. It brings together extracts from Merton's *Asian Journal* ("Hinduism" and "Varieties of Buddhism") and from other short works on Eastern religions written in the last few years of his life. They all combine to demonstrate the breadth of vision that is such an integral part of Merton's lasting appeal, his quest for a deeper unity underlying apparent fragmentation. They might be regarded as steps toward the great book on monasticism that Merton might have written but never did. As they stand, they provide Merton's essential definitions of the religions that so much interested him in the last years of his life, and of which he became the most skillful Western interpreter.

Also published by Burns & Oates

LISTEN TO THE DESERT
Secrets of Spiritual Maturity from the Desert Fathers
Gregory Mayers

"The Wisdom of the Desert," in the form of collections of sayings from the men and women who sought refuge in the Egyptian deserts from the cares and snares of the world some 1,500 years ago, exercises a lasting fascination.

These sayings can also provide a thoroughly contemporary resource for facing the challenges of the modern world, as Fr Gregory Mayers shows in this compelling book. Each chapter is introduced by a "saying," which is then expounded and worked into a highly relevant exercise in spiritual development. Fr Mayers brings his training in psychology and the Western tradition of contemplative practice, together with studies in Zen and long experience in directing retreats, to one of the most original and profound works of "spiritual direction" to appear for many years.

In fresh language, devoid of religious jargon and technicalities, Gregory Mayers sets out to show, no less, that "what has traditionally been labelled 'mysticism' and as such reserved for the rare 'worthy' individual is, in reality, the common heritage and full flowering of Christianity, and therefore ought to be accessible to all of us." This book is an invitation to the journey of self-discovery and the greater discovery of the "unknowable *that* called Love."

Burns & Oates publish books of general Christian interest, theology, scripture studies, lives of saints and works of and on mysticism and spirituality.
A free catalogue will be sent on request.
Burns & Oates Dept. A,
Wellwood, North Farm Road, Tunbridge Wells, Kent TN2 3DR, England
Tel (01892) 510850   Fax (01892) 515903